LYCRA

The Anthropology of Stuff is part of a new series, *The Routledge Series for Creative Teaching and Learning in Anthropology*, dedicated to innovative, unconventional ways to connect undergraduate students and their lived concerns about our social world to the power of social science ideas and evidence. Our goal is to help spark social science imaginations and in doing so, open new avenues for meaningful thought and action. Each 'Stuff' title is a short text illuminating for students the network of people and activities that create their material world.

Lycra describes the development of a specific fiber, but in the process provides students with rare insights into U.S. corporate history, the changing image of women in America, and how a seemingly doomed product came to occupy a position never imagined by its inventors and contained in the wardrobe of virtually every American. And it will generate lively discussion of the story of the relationship between technology, science and society over the past half a century.

Kaori O'Connor is a Research Fellow in the Department of Anthropology, University College London (UCL) in the United Kingdom. She holds four degrees in anthropology, worked on *Vogue* magazine, was the founding editor of the *Fashion Guide to London*, has written several books on fashion and shopping, designed hand knitwear and originated and presented fashion and lifestyle features for television, radio and national newspapers. She also works on the anthropology of food, for which she won the 2009 Sophie Coe Prize for her study of the Hawaiian Luau. Her most recent book is *The English Breakfast: The Biography of a National Meal* published by Kegan Paul.

The Routledge series for Creative Teaching and Learning in Anthropology

Editor: Richard H. Robbins, SUNY at Plattsburgh

This Series is dedicated to innovative, unconventional ways to connect under-graduate students and their lived concerns about our social world to the power of social science ideas and evidence. Our goal is to help spark social science imaginations and in doing so, open new avenues for meaningful thought and action.

Available

Re-Imagining Milk
Andrea S. Wiley

Coffee Culture
Catherine M. Tucker

Forthcoming

Fake Stuff
China and the rise of counterfeit goods
Yi-Chieh Jessica Lin

Reading the iPod as an Anthropological Artifact
Lane DeNicola

LYCRA

How a Fiber Shaped America

Kaori O'Connor

Routledge
Taylor & Francis Group

NEW YORK AND LONDON

First published 2011
by Routledge
270 Madison Avenue, New York, NY 10016

Simultaneously published in the UK
by Routledge
2 Park Square, Milton Park, Abingdon, Oxon OX14 4RN

Routledge is an imprint of the Taylor & Francis Group, an informa business

Typeset in Baskerville by Wearset Ltd, Boldon, Tyne and Wear
Printed and bound in the United States of America on acid-free paper by Walsworth Publishing Company, Marceline, MO

Library of Congress Cataloging in Publication Data
O'Connor, Kaori.
Lycra / Kaori O'Connor.
p. cm. – (The Routledge series for creative teaching and learning in anthropology)
1. Sport clothes industry–History. 2. E.I. du Pont de Nemours & Company–History. 3. Baby boom generation–History. I. Title.
HD9948.5.D87O26 2011
338.7'687–dc22   2010037391

ISBN13: 978-0-415-80436-3 (hbk)
ISBN13: 978-0-415-80437-0 (pbk)
ISBN13: 978-0-203-82990-5 (ebk)

IN MEMORIAM

With Love and Thanks

Gail Margaret Kelly
Professor of Anthropology, Reed College

Rodney Needham
Professor of Social Anthropology, University of Oxford

Owen Ulph
Professor of History, Reed College

Peter Gathercole
Cambridge University Museum of Archaeology and Anthropology

CONTENTS

ILLUSTRATIONS

Figures

Table

SERIES FOREWORD

The premise of these short books on the anthropology of stuff is that stuff talks, that written into the biographies of everyday items of our lives – coffee, T-shirts, computers, iPods, flowers, drugs, coffee and so forth – are the stories that make us who we are and that make the world the way it is. From their beginnings, each item bears the signature of the people who extracted, manu-factured, picked, caught, assembled, packaged, delivered, purchased and dis-posed of it. And in our modern market-driven societies, our lives are dominated by the pursuit of stuff.

Examining stuff is also an excellent way to teach and learn about what is exciting and insightful about anthropological and sociological ways of knowing. Students, as with virtually all of us, can relate to stuff, while, at the same time, discovering through these books that it can provide new and fasci-nating ways of looking at the world.

Stuff, or commodities and things, are central, of course, to all societies, to one extent or another. Whether it is yams, necklaces, horses, cattle or shells, the acquisition, accumulation and exchange of things is central to the identi-ties and relationships that tie people together and drive their behavior. But never, before now, has the craving for stuff reached the level it has; and never before have so many people been trying to convince each other that acquiring more stuff is what they most want to do. As a consequence, the creation, con-sumption and disposal of stuff now threatens the planet itself. Yet, to stop or even slow down the manufacture and accumulation of stuff would threaten the viability of our economy, on which our society is built.

This raises various questions. For example, what impact does the compul-sion to acquire stuff have on our economic, social and political well-being, as well as on our environment? How do we come to believe that there are certain things that we must have? How do we come to value some commodities or form of commodities above others? How have we managed to create commod-ity chains that link peasant farmers in Colombia or gold miners in Angola to wealthy residents of New York or teenagers in Nebraska? Who comes up with the ideas for stuff and how do they translate those ideas into things for people to buy? Why do we sometimes consume stuff that is not very good for us? These short books examine such questions, and more.

Few describe the extent to which our culture, social lives and history are inscribed on stuff better than Kaori O'Connor and her story of Lycra. Knowing the story of Lycra gives insights into US corporate history, and how a major corporation transformed its image from that of a maker of munitions to the producer of women's undergarments. It explains how the image and place of women in American society underwent a profound transformation and how the meanings of body shape and gender changed. It tells the story of how what seemed to be a doomed product came to occupy a place that its designers never imagined. It is also the story of the relationship between technology, science and society over the past half-century. And all this is written on a fabric contained in much of what we wear, whether we know it or not.

Richard Robbins
Series Editor

PREFACE

This is the story of a fiber that shaped America, and was shaped by it in return. At the heart of the narrative is a trinity that embraces commodity, production and consumption. They are the synthetic stretch fiber, Lycra; E.I. du Pont de Nemours and Company (Dupont), the transnational corporation that invented and developed the fiber; and the 'Babyboomers', the cohort born between 1945 and 1965, the generation for whom Lycra was created. By following all three across time and space, the study shows that stuff doesn't 'just happen', and demonstrates how the mass-produced goods that make up our material world are originated, produced, marketed, consumed, accepted or rejected as a result of the interplay of complex and constantly changing political, economic, ideological, technological, cultural and historical factors and processes. Until recently, stuff has been widely seen as superficial, trivial and peripheral to economics, politics, business and society. Now it is becoming clear that the opposite is the case, and it is only by understanding how stuff like Lycra comes into being and enters or leaves everyday life that we can fully understand the dynamics of our increasingly complex world, and our place within it.

This Lycra study touches on the key issues, processes and institutions of contemporary society – capitalism, commodification, commodity chains, corporations, corporate culture, social change, gender/sexuality, age, embodiment, identity, demography, production, consumption and public culture – but it does so in an innovative and distinctively anthropological way, starting from the following three premises.

1   Capitalism is a cultural system, not just an economic or political one.
2   Commodities are social values in material form.
3   Production and consumption are socially constructed.

The resultant narrative is a work of 'thick description', that goes far beyond the conventional perception of production as the simple pursuit of profit, and consumption as mere personal gratification. A unique feature of the analysis is that it begins, not with the straightforward study of stuff, but the study of 'stuff that isn't there' – a pair of Lycra aerobics leggings, of the kind that were 'fashionable' in the 1980s, but were no longer available in the present even though there was a demand for them. Looking at stuff that isn't there – or stuff that should and could be there, or was there once but isn't now – gives a far more dynamic and nuanced view of society, process and changing ideologies and values than material culture alone. It allows us to look beneath the surface, to ask deeper questions about why things are the way they are.

Somewhat unusually for an anthropological study, this work 'studies up', not down. It looks at elites rather than the powerless, at the mainstream rather than the margins, uses collective representations and cohorts rather than relying on small groups, links different times and places, deals with mass production and consumption rather than small scale, and mixes ethnography with archival work on the Dupont papers held at the Hagley Museum and Library in Wilmington, Delaware, where the 'inside' story of Lycra can be traced from before it came into being. If anthropology does not develop in this direction, we cannot hope to fully understand or contribute to the world in which we live.

After the Introduction, Chapter 2 shows how Dupont family history and values gave rise to a strong corporate culture and distinctive business practices that ultimately resulted in a wide range of diversified mass-market products that influenced everyday life on an unprecedented scale. Chapter 3 focuses on one of Dupont's diversified divisions – Textile Fibers – and the way the company identified itself with the emerging women's market, creating new chemical fibers for modern life, and altering their corporate image in the process. Chapter 4 follows Dupont's efforts to invent the holy grail of textile fibers – the perfect girdle. Lycra was developed for the purpose, and launched in 1959 after twenty years of research and development, but soon sales of the new Lycra girdles plummeted as the young Boomer women of the 1960s abandoned the girdle despite Dupont's efforts to save it. Chapter 5 charts the re-emergence of Lycra in the sweeping social changes of the Women's Movement, when the fiber that had been invented for the restrictive girdles that symbolized women's controlled position in society now became the fiber of liberation when made up into aerobic leotards and leggings worn by women reinventing themselves and their bodies. Chapter 6 catches up with the Boomers, Lycra and Dupont in the present, and offers a provocative explanation for why the original Lycra leotards 'weren't there'. Taken together, the chapters show what anthropology and stuff can contribute to understanding capitalism and contemporary life 'at home'.

I had the great good fortune to be taught by the four people to whom this book is dedicated. In their different ways, they taught me five important rules:

keep your eyes and ears open; keep your mind open; aim for clarity and simplicity not jargon and obfuscation; don't be afraid to try new things; and, above all, learn to think for yourself. Whatever the subject or discipline, this is what education should be about, and I hope I have been able to pass on some of it in this study of Lycra. The object of this series is to generate new insights, develop new theories, challenge established paradigms, and encourage innovative work. For that reason, I have presented the Lycra narrative in as non-determined a manner as possible, in order to highlight new possibilities and perspectives, and show what can be achieved by approaching the field creatively. The theory and critical thought are there, but beneath the surface, not dictating how you should interpret or develop the material presented. I want you to build on this narrative, critique or reinterpret it, or best of all go off and do something entirely new yourself. Life is an adventure, anthropology is a wonderful companion, so take those five rules, get into your metaphysical Lycra – and go for it.

ACKNOWLEDGMENTS

This study was carried out with the assistance and support of many organizations and individuals, to whom I am deeply grateful. The research was funded by the Economic and Social Research Council (ESRC) of Great Britain (Grant PTA-026–27–0089), and by further research grants from the Center for the History of Business, Technology and Society at Hagley, Wilmington, Delaware, and the Pasold Research Fund of the UK. The study could not have been undertaken without the cooperation of E.I. du Pont de Nemours and Company and the help and generosity of the Hagley Museum and Library, to both of which I owe a great debt of thanks, especially to Marge McNinch, Carol Lockman and Jon Williams of Hagley. The work was carried out under the auspices of the Department of Anthropology, University College London (UCL), where the support and encouragement of Daniel Miller, Philip Burnham and Allen Abramson were invaluable. I am grateful to my series editor Richard Robbins, to my publisher Steve Rutter, and to Leah Babb-Rosenfeld of Routledge for bringing the book into being; to my reviewers – Sharon Zukin, Carol Mukhopadhyay and Mary King – for their insightful comments; to the countless members of the Boomer cohort who contributed so much along the way; to my wonderful aunt Martha Yamashiro, and last but not least to my beloved daughter Kira Eva Tokiko Kalihilihiokekaiokanaloa Ffion Lusela Hopkins, for being herself.

Note on Dupont Nomenclature

There are many variants of the Dupont name. The legal name of the corporation is E.I. du Pont de Nemours and Company, which over time has been rendered variously as Dupont, Du Pont, du Pont, duPont and DuPont. Family members also use different spellings of the surname. In this work, it has not been possible to standardize usage, and different spellings in the text reflect the sources from which they have been drawn.

1

INTRODUCTION
Lycra, the Ethnographic Moment and the Anthropology of Stuff

The woman who brushed past me in the sports section of a large department store was fifty-something, overweight and wearing the expression of someone who was having a Bad Shopping Day. She looked so out of place among the life-size posters of world class athletes and large flatscreens showing even younger people engaging in extreme sports to the sounds of Indie music that no one comes to serve her, presumably thinking – if they noticed her at all – that she had wandered into the wrong department and would soon leave. The woman began to work her way through the racks of sports clothes, snatching hangers from the rails, examining them and shoving them back with mounting annoyance. Sports clothes in stretchy Lycra, many of which had been on display for so long that they had been marked down in price several times, surrounded her. There were cycling shorts, crop tops, bright stirrup pants with go-fast stripes down the sides, shiny zip-fronted all-in-ones that looked like surfer's wetsuits or bondage gear, thong-bottomed leotards and fluorescent separates with holes in strange places, designed to show off every angle of a young and perfectly toned body, but nothing met with her approval. The woman managed to attract the attention of a sales assistant. The phrases 'need them', 'aerobics', 'like I used to have', 'Jane Fonda' and, finally, 'I want to speak to the manager' rose shrilly above the music. Twenty-five at most, and a gym regular judging from the physique revealed by his figure-hugging t-shirt, the sportswear manager listened to the woman's complaint. After her doctor told her she should be taking regular exercise at her age, she explained, she had visited many shops in search of size-18 Lycra leotards and leggings to work out in, and so had her friends. She pointed at the crowded racks, on which hung nothing larger than a small size 10, nothing long, nothing plain. Why, she demanded, couldn't she find what she and her friends were looking for? The manager shrugged. 'I'm sorry, there's no call for it.' Even as he said it, I realized I had overheard exchanges like this before. I knew there *was* a call for large leotards and leggings in Lycra. So what was going on?

The Ethnographic Moment

'Ethnographic moments' – for this is what I was experiencing – are flashes of anthropological insight that make the strange familiar and the familiar strange. Something about ethnographic moments 'don't make sense', 'aren't right', 'don't add up' and generally demand explanation. The significance of the ethnographic moment is not always apparent at the beginning. It matters, but you don't know how or why. The experience can be compared to stumbling upon the answer, and then having to find out what the question is. You do it by starting with the moment itself, reducing it to its component parts, and following them where they lead, hoping they will all meet up in the end and make the meaning of the moment clear. Counterintuitive though they may seem, ethnographic moments often provide innovative insights into the world behind everyday appearances because they break down the naturalized values and associations and taken-for-granted beliefs that keep us from seeing what is really happening around us. So what about the Lycra leotard and leggings in size 18?

The woman I had seen looking for large workout clothes was as unfamiliar to me as she was to the sports department manager. As an anthropologist specializing in fashion 'at home' in our society, I had worked on *Vogue* magazine, been the founding editor of *The Fashion Guide* to London, designed clothes and written popular books on fashion and design. My primary fieldwork site was the Size Zero, always-youthful world of catwalks, gilt chairs, fashion shows, press releases, champagne, goodie bags, exclusive boutiques and salons, magazine deadlines, luxury fabrics, designers, photographers and the model faces-of-the-moment. A world far removed from mass-produced goods, mid-market chain stores and women who looked their age. Yet the ethnographic moment continued to nag at me.

In luxury fashion, scarcity only enhances the value and cachet of designer goods like Louboutin shoes and Chanel accessories – the waiting lists for 'Birkin' handbags by Hermes is allegedly two years long – but I had always assumed that, outside the luxury market, demand and supply met up in a fairly straightforward way. Yet the ethnographic moment had revealed women with money to spend walking away from shops empty-handed because the stuff they wanted wasn't available – even though it should have been. Leotards and leggings are design classics so there were no style changes to deal with. The women wanted them in black, so there was no problem with fashion colors. Lycra stretches, so fit wasn't going to be an issue. Compared to high-fashion clothes, it seemed to me that nothing could be simpler than supplying large, plain, black Lycra leotards and leggings. Intrigued, I began to look out for them on a casual basis when I was in shops and stores in different cities, but found nothing. This made less and less sense, especially since – as I was now becoming aware – there were many more size-18 women than Size-Zero women, and many more women between the ages of forty-five and sixty-four than I was accustomed to seeing in fashion boutiques and magazines. Other questions began to emerge. Just what was it that these women valued – Lycra's hold on their bodies, or on their memories? Was it the physical qualities of Lycra, the way it made them look and feel when they wore it? Or did it remind them of another period in their lives, epitomized for many by Jane Fonda, whose name came up again and again among midlife women looking for Lycra leggings? I found myself thinking more about 'stuff' and especially about the stuff people wear.

The Anthropology of Stuff

Stuff doesn't just happen. But exactly how and why does stuff come into being as part of the everyday material world that surrounds and defines us individually, socially, locally and globally? Standard explanations usually involve three out of the 'Four C's' of contemporary life – Capitalism, Corporations and Consumption. It is impossible to understand the modern world without an understanding of the capitalist economy (Robbins 2011). The standard explanatory model is one in which a capitalist profit imperative drives labor in the service of corporations to produce more and more goods for people to consume, in order to generate profits that go back to capitalist investors, who then start the cycle all over again. But is that really all there is to it?

All too often, and especially in the hands of economic and business historians such as Joseph Schumpeter and Alfred D. Chandler Jr., studies of corporations have focused on generalized organizational structure and 'scientific' management techniques, rather than on the idiosyncrasies of particular corporations or the things that particular corporations produce. They also present corporations as wholly logical and rational enterprises, motivated only by profit, unaffected by the perceived irrationalities of fashion, fads or public sentiment. If this were true, a large market for goods that were not being supplied simply couldn't exist, but I had found just that in the case of the large-size Lycra leggings that *should* have been there – and weren't.

Another popular model – Annie Leonard's wide-ranging online *The Story of Stuff* (2007) – concentrates on consumers and on everyday life rather than on corporations, following a four-stage trajectory of extraction–production–distribution–consumption to see, as she puts it, where the stuff we buy comes from, and where it goes when we throw it out. Exploitation, misrepresentation and pollution lurk all along the line. 'It didn't just happen. It was designed', Leonard warns – but why and by whom is never explicit. Leonard performs the valuable service of returning conscience to the equation, making people think about the social and environmental consequences of consumption choices on a global scale. But that is not the same thing as understanding how stuff happens. Or doesn't.

Why do some things get made, while others don't? Why do the things that get made take the form they do? Why are some things successful while others fail? Who thought these things up in the first place, how and why? What happens to these things over time – not after they are thrown out, but when they are still in use? Do they change their use and appearance, or do they remain the same? And what do all of these tell us about human life and the societies in which we live? These are among the questions posed by the anthropology of stuff generally and my ethnographic moment in particular. In order to answer, another 'C' was needed – Culture.

'Culture', Sir Edward Burnett Tylor, one of the founders of anthropology, wrote in 1873, '...taken in its broad, ethnographic sense, is that complex whole which includes knowledge, belief, art, morals, law, custom, and any other capabilities and habits acquired by man as a member of society.' Tylor saw society in holistic terms, as a totality comprised of interconnected parts. By studying the thoughts, beliefs, arts, creations and customs of peoples, and the similarities and differences between them, Tylor argued, anthropologists could gain insights into particular societies and then into all humankind. Material objects or stuff played a central role in this project. Observing the things people made, how they were used and valued, and what they meant to those concerned, enabled anthropologists to see things as the 'natives' saw them, and gain an understanding of how each society worked. This approach served well enough in the small-scale and isolated societies that the first anthropologists studied, but less so as time went on, especially when applied to developing societies and those of contemporary Europe and the United States where diversity, modernity, largeness of scale, mass production, migration, global capitalism, the rate of social change and a postcolonial rethinking of anthropology itself (Ortner 1984) among other factors had, by the 1950s, proved too challenging for the old culture concept in the eyes of many. What light could the red powder used in Zande witchcraft or old shell necklaces from Melanesia throw on everyday life in the world's most advanced capitalist nations?

Lots, according to Horace Miner, who in 1956 published a stylish satirical defense of cultural anthropology entitled *Body Rituals of the Nacirema,* now available online. In it, Miner described the magical beliefs and exotic practices of a tribe that spent much of their time engaged in economic activity, and much of the profits from these activities on ceremonies and rituals focused on the human body, revealing an obsession with the mouth and with the size of female breasts, and blind faith in the infallibility of medicine men. In the end, the Nacirema are revealed to be Americans (read 'Nacirema' backwards), and the essay a penetrating commentary on the strangeness of contemporary practices and beliefs about beauty, morality and medicine in American society that are taken for granted as being 'normal', insights uniquely gained by adopting a cultural perspective.

Despite the Nacirema, the holism that had been at the core of the anthropological project began to break down. 'Culture' and 'society' steadily parted company as those seeking to 'de-exoticize' anthropology and, as they saw it, bring it into the mainstream of social studies, focused on political and economic issues. In their hands, as Ortner (1984: 140) pointed out, 'culture was converted to "ideology" and considered from the point of view of its role in social reproduction: legitimating the existing order, mediating contradictions in the base, and mystifying the sources of exploitation and inequality in the system'. At first it was thought ideologies and the flow of power emanated from institutions like corporations and the state, although later the more nuanced concept of 'controlling processes' emerged in which there is 'a link between ideas, institutions and human agency whereby power is double-edged and simultaneously centered and decentered' (Nader 1997: 711). This later view was, as Sahlins (1999) pointed out, not unlike the old culture concept, but partial, and only phased in political terms. New subfields of critical political/economic anthropology arose. The study of stuff gave way to the analysis of ideas, the politics of socioeconomic relations and the inequalities of gender and production. As the trend continued, 'society' came to be seen as 'where the action was ... real politics and real economics' (Sahlins 1999: 401), while 'culture' was increasingly devalued, dismissed and marginalized, coming to be thought of as the abstract icing on the real cake of society, contingent on and peripheral to what really mattered.

In the 1970s, these developments were decried and resisted in different ways by two anthropologists in particular, Dame Mary Douglas and Marshall Sahlins. Both had done important work 'at home' in the United States and Europe. Both believed that cultural anthropology could make unique and important contributions to understanding contemporary life in the mainstream of advanced capitalism, and saw culture and society as inseparable. As Douglas put it – what good is one shoe without the other?

Both were struck by the rising tide of stuff that was engulfing everyday life under capitalism, a phenomenon that critical theory could not fully explain. Like the children in Hans Christian Anderson's tale *The Emperor's New Clothes*, Sahlins and Douglas persisted in posing the core questions of cultural anthropology that it had now become unfashionable to ask. Profit and exploitation were all very well, but why this stuff in particular, not other stuff? Who was using it and how? Who was producing it and why? And what did this say about capitalist societies, and society as a whole?

Just when things seemed darkest for cultural anthropology, stuff came to the rescue. Disembodied ideologies had proved difficult to follow, but things were not. The publication of *The Social Life of Things* edited by Arjun Appadurai (1986: 5) signaled the start of an interdisciplinary field of study that focused on 'the stuff of material culture', returning it to a central position in understanding the way we live in an era of globalization. Attracting anthropologists, archaeologists, historians, art historians, sociologists, designers, and economic and business historians among others, the new study of stuff is about the social meaning material goods have for us, how they come to have these meanings, how these meanings change as the goods move across time and space, how social meanings are translated into economic values, how the goods and meanings and values attached to them circulate, in specific contexts and historical periods. Among the most influential of these new works was Sidney Mintz's *Sweetness and Power* (1985), which followed the commodity sugar across time and space, showing how it transformed social relations and consumption patterns, and was transformed by them in return.

A particularly valuable method devised by the anthropologist Igor Kopytoff has been that of preparing a 'cultural biography of a thing', phrased by him in terms that are easily accessible to non-anthropologists:

> In doing the biography of a thing, one would ask questions similar to those one asks about people: What, sociologically, are the biographical possibilities inherent in its 'status' and in the period and culture, and how are these possibilities realized? Where does the thing come from and who made it? What had been its career so far, and what do people consider to be an ideal career for such things? What are the recognized 'ages' or periods in the thing's 'life', and what are the cultural markers for them? How does the thing's use change with its age, and what happens to it when it reaches the end of its usefulness?
>
> (Kopytoff 1986: 66)

I could answer all these questions at the drop of a designer original hat – but only as long as I remained in the small arena of luxury fashion, focusing on exclusive things that, by definition, had a pedigree. When it came to more ordinary mass-produced clothing – black leggings and leotards in Lycra, size 18 – I was at a loss. I resolved to construct a cultural biography of Lycra, but what anthropological guidelines could I follow?

Very few anthropologists have worked on contemporary mainstream dress in the United States or Europe (Hansen 2004), but as I brooded on my ethnographic moment, I remembered Sahlins' work on American clothing. In *Culture and Practical Reason*, written in the heat of his 1970s advocacy of the inseparability of culture and society, Sahlins used mass-produced American clothing to suggest how capitalist economies can be seen as *cultural* systems. His object was not to replace 'economy' with 'culture', but to return to anthropological holism, and to see them as parts of an interdependent whole.

The elite made-to-order outfits of high-fashion couture were not relevant to Sahlins' model: only mass-produced garments in common use could throw light on broad social groupings and processes in the context of high capitalism. Using garments such as doctors' coats, toddlers' outfits and the different kinds of clothes and accessories that are considered suitable for young women and for older women, he showed how mass-produced goods can be seen as a 'virtual map of the cultural universe', with the meaningful differences in types of clothes corresponding to important socio-cultural distinctions between, for example, different social classes, genders and ages. With social change, new kinds of clothes come into being, or existing ones are appropriated and given new meanings – as in the 1960s, when middle-class youth culture adopted denim work clothes as a sign of rebellion against white-collar conformity.

Economists would call this the law of supply and demand, but that can't account for the specificities of what gets produced and consumed, and how. In *The Fashion System*, Barthes (1985: 297) claimed that 'fashion is sustained by certain producer groups in order to precipitate the renewal of clothing', begging the question of who these groups are, or how they are able to precipitate renewal. Sahlins cautioned against such simplistic 'explanations'. The American mass-produced clothing system, he said, was 'not the generation of demand by supply, as though the social product were the conspiracy of a few decision makers able to impose an ideology of fashion through the deceits of advertising', nor 'the converse mystification of capitalist product as a response to consumer wants'. It was the materialization of a cultural logic, the outcome of culture and society working upon and through each other, and influencing producers and consumers alike.

Sahlins suggested that an in-depth study of mass-produced clothing could reveal in more detail how stuff embodies cultural values or ideologies; what these values or ideologies are; how social change is reflected in stuff and vice versa, and how producers and consumers are involved in the process. He even outlined the field resources available for such a study – all the participants in the fashion process, including advertising professionals, market researchers, designers, buyers, fashion editors and critics, consumers and the producers themselves. It was, I thought, the ideal blueprint for a study by an anthropologist who was also a fashion editor, of a puzzling commodity on the cusp between culture and economy that posed questions that went straight to the heart of Sahlins' work: where had Lycra leggings come from, where had they gone and why, and what did the whole process tell us? In the years since it had been written, no one had explored the territory Sahlins had signposted in depth. The field was open and the need for a study of this kind – as indicated by Lycra leggings and my ethnographic moment – was greater than ever.

Over the past two decades, much interdisciplinary work has been done on consumption as identity, shopping (notably Zukin's ethnographically rich and insightful 2004 study, *Point of Purchase*), and the construction of the self through choice. One of the assumptions about the 'post-Fordian' economy in which we now live is that it provides us with infinite choice and limitless variety, but if the production of goods is culturally determined as Sahlins suggested, then choice cannot be infinite, because only certain goods are produced. If variety were truly limitless, there would have been no trouble finding large Lycra leotards and leggings.

In addition, since Sahlins had first written on clothing, a vast and variable literature on contemporary 'dress' and its 'meanings' has arisen, mainly within the fields of cultural studies, design history and fashion theory. As a fashion editor, what struck me about much of this work was how divorced it was from dress as a business. This was a gap that needed to be filled, and the study outlined by Sahlins presented an opportunity to do so. Only one aspect of Sahlins' work on clothing had previously failed to appeal to me – his interest in mass production. But finally the challenge proved irresistible, so I left high fashion behind and followed Sahlins into the material world of the mass market, in order to get to the bottom of the large Lycra leggings that weren't there.

Deconstructing the Ethnographic Moment: Cohort, Clothing, Cloth and Company

The Boomer Cohort

The mass market involves thinking and working on a vast scale, the very opposite of the exclusive luxury market, and also the very opposite of much recent work in anthropology, which has focused on diversity, difference and ever-smaller groups.

Because she was fifty-something, the woman shopping for large Lycra workout clothes was a member of a specific birth cohort – the so-called 'Babyboomers' or 'Boomers'. Born in America and the developed world between 1945 and 1964, the Boomers are the largest birth cohort in history, and therefore potentially the largest mass market in history, with some seventy-seven million born during this period in the United States alone. Which of these seventy-seven million was the woman shopper of my ethnographic moment? She could have been an English/ Scottish grandmother from Maine, a recently retired bookseller and joint owner with her husband of a mortgage-free three-bedroom house, who reads *Yankee Magazine*, likes quilting and drives a year-old Toyota. Or a German/Hispanic from south Texas, born in 1961, who operates a grapefruit farm with her same-sex partner, has a mortgage, drives a reconditioned Dodge pickup truck with a National Rifle Association sticker on the rear window and reads the *National*

Enquirer. Or an African-American from Oakland, a divorced office manager who lives in a rented apartment, uses public transport, attends church three times a week and subscribes to *O – The Oprah Magazine.* As these three examples alone show, at this level of diversity and difference, it becomes difficult to speak of anything but very small groups or even individuals. It also becomes virtually impossible to analyze society as a whole, or to examine larger social processes.

For this reason, some anthropologists are calling for a turn away from micro-studies, fragmentation and a reliance on face-to-face ethnography toward macro-studies of large groups in the population, drawing on an expanded anthropology in which ethnography and theory are combined with 'public culture', which includes representations, film, television, books, magazines, journalism, academic studies and material culture or stuff. What used to be disapproved of as 'generalizations' are becoming acceptable and even desirable, and are now known as 'collective representations'. Of course, every individual is by definition unique, but in studying 'society' we have to be able to work with individuals in their social environment, and with collective behavior over time. The anthropological project, as Douglas (1992: ix) put it, 'calls for a holistic view, over a long enough stretch of generations and over a large enough number of people, for a pattern to appear'.

This approach is not new. During World War II, a great deal of anthropological work was done on what was called 'the study of culture at a distance' (Mead and Métraux 1953). Somewhat controversially, it involved analyzing the cultural regularities and characteristics of societies such as Japan and Germany that were inaccessible to direct observation due to war. Instead of carrying out face-to-face ethnography, anthropologists used secondary sources to study such things as attitudes to the body, senses of smell and touch, definitions of friendship, films, literature, even different ways of playing chess, all in the service of what today would be called cultural profiling. After the war, anthropologists returned to ethnographic studies of small-scale societies abroad, and many anthropologists working 'at home' today continue to use face-to-face ethnographic methods developed for use in these small societies which had no indigenous films, literature, media or industrially mass-produced goods. The continued use of this approach cannot be justified in our large and complex digital society, where so much information is in virtual and mass-media circulation – where more and more people, organizations and companies engage in constructing visual and textual representations on a daily basis; and where, increasingly, less communication takes place face-to-face.

'Cohort analysis' is another form of collective representation. Originally developed by anthropologists to study traditional societies with formal age grades – groups such as 'children', youths', 'warriors' and 'elders' – it was later appropriated and developed by sociologists, social demographers and market researchers, as we will see in Chapter 4. It is a good example of how anthropology can be adapted by other disciplines and professions. Cohort analysis is based on the premise that because cohorts proceed through the age strata at different points in historical time, each is affected by historical events in a unique way (Keith and Kertzer 1984: 31; Kertzer and Fricke 1997), giving each cohort a unique history, values and cultural profile. These are the cohorts of the present era in the United States (Table 1.1) as they were in 2002 when fieldwork was being carried out.

Ortner's study of 'Generation X' is a pioneering work in the new anthropology of collective representations that uses cohort analysis. The term 'Generation X' refers to those members of the American population born between 1965 and 1976, the cohort that followed the Boomers. As a group, members of this cohort are popularly believed to be 'slackers' and 'whiners', willing to be supported by their parents, and unmotivated to find work. Ortner used aggregate data, historical materials, collective representations and ethnography to explore the questions of who and what 'Generation X' were, how their collective representation had come into being and taken on meanings and attributes, and what the representation of Generation X said about the larger culture in which it was situated. She drew particularly on 'public culture – all the products of art and entertainment, film, television, books, texts of information and analysis, and all the products of the media' (Ortner 1999: 414). Ortner (2003) concluded that representations of Generation X are a projection of anxieties arising from socioeconomic changes in American society

Cohort	Born	Age in 2002	Population size (in 1,000s)	% US population
G.I. generation	pre-1930	73+	20,515	7.3
Depression generation	1930–1939	63–72	19,144	6.8
World War II babies	1940–1945	57–62	15,323	5.5
Baby Boomers	1946–1964	38–56	77,610	27.7
Generation X	1965–1976	26–37	45,651	16.3
Generation Y	1977–1994	8–25	71,629	25.6
Millennials	1995+	0–7	30,345	10.9

Table 1.1 Cohort chart, adapted from Busting Boomer Myths seminar, October 2002, *American Demographics*.

such as declining male wages and shrinking job markets, which diminish the opportunity for middle-class War Babies and Boomers to pass their status on to their Generation X offspring.

Although employing ethnography, Ortner's study of Generation X was not reduced to it, and I decided to approach my midlife shopper and others like her in the same way. The three women described earlier, otherwise highly diverse, are all members of the Boomer cohort, and could be looked at collectively, as 'Boomers'. For the purposes of the analysis, I would take gender as a given, and focus on women, reflecting the ethnographic moment. The female members of the Boomer cohort were subject – directly or indirectly – to the influences of the complex social changes known as 'women's liberation', the 'feminist movement' and the 'Women's Movement' as it developed in the United States in the 1960s. In order to explore and expand the use of cohort analysis in anthropological study, I decided not to complicate the issue by further dividing the study group according to class and race, for the concept of cohort cuts across these. Cohort analysis is not without its critics, and the boundaries of 'Boomer-dom' have been contested. Some say the cohort begins in 1945, others in 1946. Some argue for a 'Pre-Boomer' group of people born in 1943–1944, depending on where they grew up, especially in major cities and conurbations that were centers of cultural innovation and influence such as the San Francisco–Berkeley–Bay Area. Some treat the twenty-year cohort as a single group, others split them into two ten-year segments as 'Early Boomers' and 'Late Boomers'. Outside the United States, the postwar birthrate and economic boom began slightly later and these birth groups were shaped by different events, introducing more possible variations. However, to work with collective representations effectively you have to look for the similarities that lie beyond the differences, and take a broad and flexible approach, while focusing on a particular group within the cohort. Ortner, for example, focused on the members of her high-school graduating class and their children. I took my lead from my woman shopper. She was born in the United States at the beginning of the cohort in about 1946, and that is where I began. Following the dictates of the ethnographic moment, the study would focus primarily on the United States, with additional material from Britain to reflect American market expansion after World War II.

Looking at the Boomer cohort collectively, the most striking thing is its sheer size relative to other cohorts (see Table 1.1). Going on numbers alone, they constituted the largest potential mass market in the population, the one market that should have had no trouble in finding any goods they wanted, which made the ethnographic moment even more puzzling. The second thing that became apparent was that, more than any other birth cohort, the Boomers were defined by stuff.

In America, the baby boom coincided with the unprecedented economic boom that followed World War II. Producing for babies became a boom industry in itself for, culturally as well as numerically, these children were at the heart of postwar life. The importance of 'the family' was the dominant theme in advertising in the postwar years (Marchand 1985, 1998), and Walker (2000), using women's magazines as a primary resource, has shown how family life achieved an unparalleled prominence in the domestic arena. Boomer children – particularly those born in the first half of the cohort – received an exceptional degree of attention, from both parents and producers. They also received a remarkable amount of stuff.

When I asked Boomers what stuff they remembered from their childhoods, their answers were a virtual catalog of the fads that swept through young America in the 1950s and early 1960s – Davy Crockett coonskin caps, Mr. Potato Head, Hopalong Cassidy cap pistols, Red Flyer wagons, Howdy Doody puppets, hula hoops, Duncan yoyos with rhinestones round the edge, Barbie dolls and much, much more. As Cross (2000: 16) put it, 'Baby-boom children learned how to be consumers through their toys.' As they grew older, vanguard Boomers became the first teenage consumers, generating a wave of new goods and fashions – Pendleton shirts, net crinolines, bobby socks and penny loafers, pop beads and portable record players. Never before had a time, place and generation been so embodied in and signified by mass-produced goods – it was, after all, the cohort that became known as 'the Pepsi Generation' (Hollander and Germain 1992): the generation who took the abundance of stuff produced especially for them for granted (Lears 1994). I began to suspect that the cultural biographies of the Boomer cohort and of stuff were inextricably linked. The idea of seeing Lycra through the Boomer cohort, and the Boomer cohort through Lycra, took root.

I now had to make certain the ethnographic moment had not been a fluke. Were there really no large Lycra leggings and leotards out there, and was there actually a demand or need for them? I now began systematic retail ethnography – lurking in shops and stores in order to see what the shop was selling and how it was being displayed, working out the ambience and 'personality' of the shop, profiling the shop's target or ideal customers, observing the way customers were treated, and seeing what promotional activities and tie-ins the shop was involved in. Very soon, I found myself seized by a strong sense of déjà-vu as the ethnographic moment repeated itself. No matter if the shop was a department in a large store or a stand-alone establishment, a smart specialty store or a discount outlet, whether in the middle of a town or city or at a suburban mall, and whether there was a lot of stock or a smaller, select range – there were no large Lycra leotards or leggings in size 18.

I began to quiz the staff. Was I the only person who had asked them for large leggings and leotards? Did they ever have them in stock and, if so, who bought them? I got a lot of shrugs and dismissive reactions, one young man saying what many of the others obviously thought – that size 18 50+ women shouldn't wear leotards and leggings. Older staff tended to be more sympathetic. One admitted that she got asked for them 'all the time', and another said wistfully, 'I'm on commission and I could sell a lot, if only we had them in stock.' One suggested, 'Why don't you look on the Internet?' A trawl of the Net revealed that 'plus size' sweats were available for men, but not for women, while a few mail-order dance suppliers had Lycra leotards in what they called Size XL, but which were actually more like a Size 14 at best. In any case, I didn't see why something so basic, with such a large potential market, wasn't available in shops anyone could just walk into.

While older staff knew what I was talking about, those who belonged to Generations X and Y were too young to remember the Lycra leotards and leggings that were popular during the Boomers' youth. One of my Boomer informants lent me a pair of aerobic leotards and tights from the 1970s, now with a few holes and too threadbare to wear – 'I don't know why I keep it, but I can't bear to throw it out' – which I began to take along with me. Inventing a mother and aunt who had been told by their doctors to take exercise, I would repeat what the woman shopper had said during the ethnographic moment, and show the staff the leotard and leggings. My mom and auntie, I would say, couldn't understand why what they wanted wasn't in the shops, and why there weren't exercise clothes for older, larger women. The sight of the vintage workout wear, and the plight of my fictional relatives, often triggered the same reaction – 'That's what my mother says'. Which was music to my ears, because the mothers of young sales staff were likely to be Boomers. So what did their mothers do about it? Apparently, they wore old leggings, sweats or joggers, but not happily. 'She's always complaining, but I don't know what the answer is,' said one, obviously tired of parental grumbling.

The answer would be to have the stuff in the shops, so I continued my quest to find out why it wasn't there. The department stores, I found, were less useful sources of information because of changes in retailing. The size of their sportswear departments had dwindled steadily over the years as more and more people went to specialist sports shops. Also, many formerly independent department stores were now part of chains, with a central buying policy that seemed to originate in a place that might as well have been on Mars as far as staff were concerned, since they now had no knowledge of what was being purchased for the store until deliveries of new stock arrived, and no in-store buyer to ask about the range. As for the merchandise, it was predominantly for street- and leisure-wear rather than for active sports or exercise. Leotards and leggings, in any size, were unknown.

Some well-known sportswear brands maintain flagship shops in major cities, establishments that combine the functions of promotional space and retail outlet. The object of these flagship shops is to publicize links with top athletes and show off the top-of-the-range branded goods, thus enhancing the value of the brand generally, and the more basic branded goods sold in ordinary outlets. Staff in these establishments are generally handpicked for their ability, looks, athletic skill and knowledge. Knowledge, I found, that was not always valued by their employers.

One particularly lavish flagship establishment I visited was more like a multi-floor temple to sport, athletic heroes and the sporting life than a shop. Giant screens with synchronized music presented an Olympian display of just about any sport you could wish to see, alongside filmed interviews with star athletes wearing clothes from the current collections displayed for sale on nearby racks. The shop was full of people, mainly jocks and gym bunnies buying things for themselves, with a fair number of dads who seemed to have been dragged in by their kids, but among the milling crowds I spotted some Boomer women, wandering uncertainly. Sidling up and initiating a conversation, I discovered that they were looking for clothes to exercise in. They hadn't found any. After more scouting around, I located a sales supervisor, showed him the vintage leggings and leotard, and went through the story about my mom and aunt. After giving me the by-now familiar response – 'My mother says that' – he went on:

> I think they let the designers go too far on the stuff we have here. It's too fashion, too extreme. This brand is about health, about fitness, not about fashion. It used to be about stuff people knew us for, and would buy over and over. Now new stuff comes in all the time. When the company gets it right, people come back wanting more, but by then it's sold out, gone, *nada*, and the designers have moved on to another look. I don't think they should do that. Everyone on the selling floors has the same experience, with people coming up to us saying where's the so-and-so, why can't I get it anymore? Like with your leggings. And when we don't have it, they walk out and we lose money. The company should listen to us, the sales staff, because we *know*. The brand is sold everywhere, but here in this flagship store is the only place you really get feedback. When they opened this store, we had a big launch event, there must have been 600 women here. The company had people going around with clipboards, asking the women what they thought of this and that, what kinds of things they wanted to buy, but it isn't the same as the day-to-day things *we* hear and see. Take your older, bigger woman. OK, maybe we don't have leggings, even though I do get asked for them. But we do have big joggers and t-shirts that can fit an 18. But all we have in the women's area are little skimpy things, fashion tops and crops. I have to tell these women to

go the men's department to get big joggers and t-shirts because that's where we keep them. But that doesn't make them feel good about themselves, having to go to the men's department, and it puts them off. They walk out, and we lose again. Those big joggers and tops are unisex anyway, there's no reason at all why we can't have a few of them in the women's area, yah. It doesn't make sense.

(Sales supervisor, brand flagship store)

Ultimately, however, designers aren't responsible for the lack of large size exercise clothes and nor are they ignorant of the contradiction between what they are asked to produce and the kind of clothes people really exercise in, as I had confirmed to me at a studio that produced prototype designs for one of the best-known American sport brands:

My boss is a Boomer, and she works out regularly. I don't know what she wears in the gym, but she's said many times that she wouldn't be caught dead working out in the exercise clothes we produce. She says they're just club clothes, pretending to be gym wear. And she could wear anything, she's in fantastic shape. I don't know what women who aren't in great shape do.

(Assistant studio designer)

So my Boomer woman shopper may not have been getting what she wanted, but did she really need it? To find out, I joined a YMCA-certified training course for fitness professionals planning to specialize in exercise for older people. Founded in London in 1844, today the YMCA is a worldwide movement with more than forty-five million members, open to all regardless of faith, social class, age or gender. YMCA gyms have an exceptionally wide community of users, ranging from children to people aged 90+, along with facilities and machines for many kinds of exercise, taught classes for everything from dance to tai chi, training courses for fitness instructors and membership fees that are low in comparison to other gyms and clubs – an ideal place to assess need and observe practice in the fitness mass market.

AOA (Active Older Adult) exercise classes are a relatively new but rapidly expanding field within professional fitness teaching, reflecting the aging of the population as the Boomer cohort gets older, and also the increasing recognition of the benefits of exercise in later life. Exercise for older people, generally defined as those aged 50+, was, I discovered, much more complex than exercise for the young. Trainee AOA teachers have to familiarize themselves with the physical limitations of the aging body and design exercise routines to accommodate them, while still pushing the aging body to maintain and extend its capabilities in the face of ongoing decline. One instructor described it to me as running to stay in the same place. AOA teachers were not interested in the aesthetics of body image, but in the problems caused by lack of exercise in later life, such as difficulty performing such everyday tasks as getting up from a chair or closing curtains, in the absence of medical conditions that might contribute to the problem. As one AOA instructor put it to me:

> So many difficulties are not age-related, they are inactivity-related. The message is simple – use it or lose it. We want to help people prolong active living and remain independent. Of course there are age-related changes, but these don't have to happen so soon or be so severe. Many people think they should do less when they are older, but this is just not true. People also think that the fitness they had in their twenties will carry them through, but it won't. You have to keep at it. I can't say it often enough, I say it to my seniors all the time. *Use it or lose it.*
>
> (AOA lead fitness training instructor)

Later, I was able to compare the YMCA with an establishment at the other end of the social scale – *Les Thermes Marins de Monte Carlo* – located in Monaco, where Dupont used to hold an event called the *Lycra Rendez-Vous* every January, for the benefit of swimsuit makers and buyers from all over the world. A seaside municipal health facility for a community of millionaires, the *Thermes* consists of a large seawater pool overlooking the sea, perfumed Turkish baths, saunas, spa treatments and physiotherapy, and a glass-walled fitness room with the latest equipment and treadmills, arranged so they survey the yacht harbor directly below. Slipping away from the young and perfect bodies modeling Lycra swimwear in the exhibition halls, I came here to see how the not-so-young but very rich kept themselves in shape. Water aerobics in the pool were favored by the local ladies of Boomer age and older, performed in one-piece structured swimsuits reminiscent of the 1950s, worn with very elaborate swimming caps: the aquatic equivalent of leggings. There is a private elevator from the marina to this health club *de luxe*, and people – deeply tanned silver-haired men predominating – would come up from their yachts to work out on the equipment, seriously and for long periods. These were people who could afford just about anything in the world, but here they were, working out just like the people in the YMCA, because at this age inner-health was more important than surface appearance. You couldn't buy it; you had to work for it. The message was the same – use it or lose it.

Back at the YMCA, the AOA instructors were not interested in gym fashion or hegemonic body image but they were very concerned indeed about function, safety and comfort. Aerobic exercise, they told the trainees, should not be carried out in bare feet, or feet in stockings only, because neither allowed exercisers to get a good grip on the floor. This was important because older people are more likely to fall over, and more likely to sustain serious injury when they do. Muscles should always be kept warm and supported, the more so as exercisers got older. Wide-bottomed pants with lots of fabric around the ankles were to be avoided, because people became less sure on their feet as they got older, and wide hems might cause the wearer to trip. It was useful for clothes to be reasonably close-fitting so the instructors could see that the joints were properly in line, important because older joints easily slip out of alignment. For these requirements, specifically tailored to the needs of AOA/Boomer exercisers, Lycra leggings and leotards would have been ideal. The exercisers in AOA classes were predominantly women; women live longer than men, so there are relatively more of them in the cohort as it ages. While older men who exercise regularly tend to prefer non-class-based activities in which Lycra leggings are not worn, such as golf, walking, work on weight-training machines or swimming, women tend to seek out exercises classes. So the potential market for leggings among midlife women definitely existed – but the leggings themselves did not.

Clothing and Cloth

Since the clothing was nowhere to be found, I decided to investigate the cloth. Because everyone wears clothes, it seems reasonable to assume that the study of cloth is a major subfield of the anthropology of stuff, and it is – up to a point. The anthropological literature is full of studies of artisanal embroidery, hand-dyed fabrics and hand-woven natural textiles from all over the world, and many periods in history. Anthropology museums are full of indigenous cloth and costumes, and the seminal work in the field, *Cloth and Human Experience* (Weiner and Schneider 1989) demonstrates that, across a wide range of cultures, 'Cloth can also communicate the ideological values and claims of the wearer or user. Complex moral and ethical issues of dominance and autonomy, opulence and poverty, continence and sexuality, find ready expression through cloth' (Weiner and Schneider 1989: 12–13). However, the cloth referred to here is traditional, handmade, natural fiber cloth, reflecting a widely held view in anthropology that only artisanal handwork and small-scale production can imbue cloth with social meaning and values.

   In the anthropological study of our own society, mass-produced and especially 'synthetic' cloth has received almost no attention. An exception is Schneider's (1994) 'In and Out of Polyester: Desire, Disdain and Global Fiber Competitions', which examines some of the negative taboos, stigmas and cultural connotations attached to synthetic fabrics in the late 1980s and early 1990s among members of the American middle- and upper-middle-class, for whom 'the word "polyester" conjured up the image of a lower middle class tour group filing off a bus in Disneyland wearing pastel leisure suits' (Schneider 1994: 2). Remembering that, in the 1950s, synthetic cloth was considered miraculous, the very embodiment of progress and modernity, Schneider asks: 'Such reversals in taste provoke a nagging question: do consumers' changing values motivate what gets produced or do producers, in possession of capital, promotional know-how and political influence, mould what consumers want?' (Schneider 1994: 2). This good question remains unresolved because Schneider's study focuses on the 'fiber wars' between the manufacturers of synthetics on the one hand, and the marketing boards for natural silk, wool and cotton fibers on the other, as reported in the trade press, mainly the journal *American Fibers and Fabrics*. Schneider does not concentrate on how synthetic cloth comes into being, or how it is consumed. Because 'polyester' is used as a catch-all term for synthetics as a whole in her study, it is difficult to get a picture of the production and consumption of individual fibers – a necessity if we are to understand how synthetic cloth becomes a commodity with complex symbolic properties, acting as McCracken (1988: 61) put it, as 'an agent of history giving cultural form and order to innovative dynamic moments'.

Lycra wasn't mentioned in Schneider's study, but I soon discovered three things about it that surprised me. First, Lycra was not a cloth or fabric as I had thought, but a fiber made of polymer chains (polyurethane polyurea copolymers) derived from petroleum, which have a complex structure that allows Lycra to stretch and to retain its shape, in degrees that can be varied to suit the product in which it is used. Beginning as a solution, Lycra is spun in drums into a fiber that is spooled and sent on to textile manufacturers who combine it with other fibers, either synthetic or natural, to give them stretch and shape retention. No garments are made of 100 percent Lycra. Second, although Lycra is so ubiquitous today that it is difficult to imagine clothing of all kinds without it, Lycra was only launched in 1959. Third, unlike polyester and many other synthetics which were and are made by all the big chemical firms and many of the smaller ones, Lycra was made by only one producer who invented it, and had strictly controlled every aspect of its production and promotion since it appeared on the market – E.I. du Pont de Nemours and Company, popularly known as 'Dupont'.

The Company at a Distance

As soon as I saw the company logo – the Dupont name in red, enclosed in an oval, also in red, against a white background – I realized it had the familiarity of something seen subliminally time and time again as part of the background of everyday life, while at the same time remaining completely unknown. I may have seen the company logo in magazine ads or on labels, but I knew nothing about the company itself.

Figure 1.1 Logo of E.I. du Pont de Nemours and Company, courtesy of Hagley Museum and
     Library.

Dupont was, I discovered, a transnational diversified corporation with a presence in some seventy countries and an annual income exceeding that of many
nation states. Although it was the oldest industrial company on the Fortune 500
list and the oldest company in the Dow Jones industrial average, Dupont did not
maintain a large presence in New York as might have been expected. Instead,
Dupont's corporate headquarters were in Wilmington, Delaware, an Atlantic
seaboard city and state that are virtually unknown outside America, and little-
known even inside it. 'Dela-where?', a common joke in the neighboring states of
Pennsylvania, New Jersey and Maryland, means nothing further afield. So under-
stated was Dupont's corporate presence – a core element in Dupont company
culture as I was to find out – that it was some time before I appreciated how
large and influential Dupont was, and how long it had been so.

   I began to study Dupont at a distance through the anthropology of public
culture and, using my fashion background, also began ethnographic observation at the major fashion fairs, textile trade fairs and textile promotional
events in which Dupont participated. Traditionally, trade fairs – held annually
or twice annually at venues around the world – have been the main arena for
all sectors of the textile trade to come together and do business. New lines of
goods will be shown, orders will be taken, new contacts made and old working
partnerships reaffirmed. Electronic systems, travel cutbacks and new forms of
sourcing and outsourcing have inevitably impacted on traditional textile fairs.
The fairs in Europe, where little large-scale textile manufacturing now takes
place, have declined, while new and highly successful fairs have sprung up in
Asia, the new textile hotspot. Overall, however, big trade fairs lasting three to
four days are still the single most important arena for fiber and fabric manufacturers to showcase their products to an international trade audience, and

for producers and buyers alike to catch up on lifestyle trends, new design technology and new supply methods. In the premier events, the major producers and manufacturers turn up with pre-fabricated stands, container-loads of samples, literature, visuals and giveaways, and a full complement of staff. Dupont had the prime position in the exhibition halls at all the fairs I attended. Their stand – more of a portable showroom/salon – was invariably the most impressive. It was beautifully designed, immaculately finished, with the most imposing displays and, above all, the best staff: smartly presented, infallibly courteous, knowledgeable and utterly professional. A central feature of the Dupont stands was a 'fabric library', with a seemingly infinite selection of fabric swatches arranged by color, by type, by weight and by fiber type, which attracted clients like flowers attract bees. There were hundreds upon hundreds of fabric samples, and Dupont staff appeared to know everything about every one of them – what kinds of garments they were best for, what kind of production methods they were suited to, what kinds of variations were available and so on. Dupont would stage fashion shows at the trade fairs, polished presentations featuring designs they had specially commissioned for the event to show off the newest fibers and fabrics, and at every fair they had new leaflets, brochures and booklets to keep clients informed of the latest developments. Their clients were loyal, their competitors treated them with respect, and they were deeply impressive to watch in action.

Yet the more I saw, the less I understood. Dupont, I came to appreciate, didn't actually make fabrics. Instead, Dupont produced the fibers which spinners, weavers and manufacturers used to make yarn, fabrics and then garments. None of the fabric samples on the Dupont stand had been made by Dupont, but by the clients who Dupont supplied with fibers. Yet even though they did not produce finished fabrics, the company was active all along the textile commodity chain, with an influence that extended beyond its direct customers. This was a unique way of working, one which did not correspond to any standard corporate model or 'rational' economic schema. It was not clear exactly how Dupont ran its textile operation, and it was not easy to find out. The company's concern for confidentiality is renowned, even in a trade that is highly secretive and specialized, and effectively closed to outsiders (Kenis 1992). Dupont does not publicize its working methods, and competitors could talk about Dupont anecdotally, but had little detailed knowledge of the company's overall methods. And beyond the 'how?' lay the 'why?'. Increasingly, it seemed to me that Dupont practices were part of a strong internal culture, which seemed to follow a private script written in the past, one which I would have to uncover in order to understand Lycra, the missing leotard and leggings, and the ethnographic moment.

The Past in the Present and Doing Anthropology in the Archives

This would involve doing anthropology in the Dupont archives. The corporate archives of E.I. du Pont de Nemours & Co and the Dupont family papers are held at the Hagley Museum and Library outside Wilmington, Delaware, which also houses the Center for the History of Business, Technology and Society. Begun as the private library of Dupont chairman Pierre S. Dupont (1870–1954), it has grown into a highly important research collection of books, manuscripts, photographs and audiovisual materials, ephemera, artifacts and company papers documenting the history of American enterprise and technology and their effect on society. The records of a number of major American companies including Avon cosmetics and Singer sewing machines are lodged at Hagley, but the largest single holding is the Dupont collection which covers two centuries and all divisions of the corporation, embracing everything from sales order books and laboratory records to minutes of meetings, departmental memoranda, newspaper cuttings, press releases, retail display materials, product samples and much more.

Archival records – like statistical data and collective representations – were formerly regarded as antithetical to ethnography and to the material gained through direct observation. Archival research was not considered 'real' anthropology. Fortunately, archives are now becoming accepted as valid ethnographic sites, with the anthropologist of the field and the present also acting as the anthropologist of the archive and the past. As the Comaroffs (1992: 11) put it: 'Ethnography surely extends beyond the range of the empirical eye: its inquisitive spirit calls upon us to ground subjective, culturally configured action in society and history and vice versa – wherever the task may take us.'

Archival research in capitalist corporations presents anthropologists with a new kind of complexity, drawing them into a hidden world of institutional papers that reveal how a company works and produces what it does. It is 'now widely accepted by historians that the sources from this private world ... [and] the structures and processes disclosed by the unpublished records constitute a reality as important as, or even more important than, the world of public utterances' (Reingold 1990). As I discovered, the collections in corporate archives can challenge much recent critical work that has been done on everyday life, query many widely held assumptions and common practices, and interrogate slippery concepts like 'ideology' and 'power'.

The sheer quantity and variety of materials available in a good corporate archive allows – indeed, forces – researchers to break through the over-reliance on advertisements which has become a feature of critical cultural analysis. In his study of advertising, O'Barr (1994: 2, 3) defines ideology as ideas 'that buttress and support a particular distribution of power in society', noting that ideology 'is political in its very nature'. In societies of advanced capitalism, advertising is deemed by critical theorists to be the primary site where the ideologies 'that support and buttress the social order of a society based on mass production and consumption' are embodied, and in recent years, much effort has been devoted to 'decoding' and 'deconstructing' the ideologies embedded in ads as a means of social analysis.

Because they are part of public culture, and therefore easily accessible through newspapers, magazines and other forms of media, advertisements have been an all-too-convenient resource for those who are unwilling or unable to work in corporate archives or observe corporations in operation at first-hand. These critiques are carried out from the perspective of the 'critical interpreter' (an academic or professional analyst) or the audience of consumers of the ads, and occasionally the designer of the ads, but not the producers of the goods that are featured in ads, despite the fact that the advertising is sponsored by and supportive of capitalism. It is assumed that the producer wants to make a profit, begging the question of why they do it in particular ways with particular goods. The justification given by O'Barr (1994: 8) is: 'Once we grasp that the consumer is the ultimate author of the meaning of an advertisement, the intentions of the makers become of secondary importance. Ultimately they may even be irrelevant.' Yet, as the materials in a full corporate archive show, to perform cultural analysis on advertisements without knowing about the producer's intentions or what was actually happening in the business, the market or society from the producer's viewpoint at the time the advertisements were commissioned and disseminated is to know only half of the story at best.

Tellingly, in a corporate archive, advertisements tend to be the least important part of the collection, with other kinds of records clearly considered more valuable by the producers themselves. Using these materials, it is possible to construct an entirely different narrative to that produced by advertising analysis, in which stuff or goods – not ideologies and visual images – play a major role. Instead of speculating about what advertisements 'meant' to audiences of consumers, corporate archives allow us to look at how and why stuff actually comes into being and is used. It may be the case that advertising 'embodies and transmits cultural beliefs, behaviors and values' (McCracken and Pollay 1981: 1), but it does not originate them and cannot perpetuate them under adverse conditions. It is only when you look at the archival record of the world of goods from the inside that you begin to appreciate the complexities that surround stuff, and the mindset of the period. For example, the virtual absence in Dupont material of the 1950s and much of the 1960s of class and all the elements of 'diversity' that we now take for granted may seem puzzling, but it is an accurate reflection of 'middle class consumerism' – the essentializing aspirational construct that was an intrinsic part of American identity at the time (Blaszczyk 2009) – that drove the rise of the technologically based mass market for much of the twentieth century, and was the way producers imagined and constructed consumers before the fragmentation of the market and the niche marketing of more recent times.

Archives raise issues about representation, access and the control of knowledge and history. Researchers must accept that no archive is ever complete, and that the material in them must be closely scrutinized for inconsistencies and misrepresentations – in the same way that field anthropologists have to evaluate what ethnographic informants tell them, and not accept fieldwork statements at face value. Also, anthropologists experienced in archival work will not rely on official records and sources alone, but will construct their own records and narratives drawn from other sources, for comparative and contextual purposes. Probably the most challenging issue – in both archival and field research, especially when working 'at home' – is that of objectivity.

A distinction that used to be common in anthropology was that between 'emic' and 'etic', terms used to distinguish two different perspectives and kinds of information arising from fieldwork. 'Emic' is the 'inside' view, culturally specific, describing how a society works as seen from the inside, and conveying what it is to be a member of that society or group: the core of ethnographic description. Going out to the field in days gone by, anthropologists would learn the language of 'their' people and stay in the field for as long as possible, in order to achieve the immersion necessary to achieving the emic perspective. 'Etic' is the 'outside' view, culturally neutral and distanced, a perspective used for comparative study and critical analysis. Periodically doubts have been expressed as to whether a fieldworker can ever be purely immersed or completely objective, but the distinction remains a useful one. Fieldwork involves both, but the balance between the two is variable, depending on the field situation, the aims of the researcher and the state of the discipline itself.

In the early days of anthropology, the emphasis was on the emic view, in order to build up information for comparative study. As time went on and comparative studies developed, the etic element gained strength and became predominant, especially after traditional isolated field sites disappeared, fieldwork periods became ever shorter and theorizing ideologies came into vogue, so much so that in some circles the emic view came to be regarded with suspicion as 'non-objective'. However, in advanced critical theory, it is now apparent that what is needed to further the understanding of 'power', 'ideology', 'culture' and 'society' under advanced capitalism is not more theory, but more ethnographic data and case studies (Drucker-Brown 1997; Robbins 2006). So, confronted by the material in the Dupont archive, the lack of comparable work and the questions posed by the ethnographic moment itself, I resolved to construct an emic account of the corporation, and of the fiber and cohort, primarily from the corporation's perspective. It is a broad approach that avoids over-determination, permits different issues and questions to emerge as the study proceeds and aims to provide material suitable for future analyses from a wide variety of specialist perspectives, as classic case studies did. As for style, I decided to follow the golden rule of fieldwork: do not impose yourself on the field; allow it to impose itself on you. So instead of the intrusive peda-gogical style favored by critical analysts, this is a narrative account in which, as far as possible, the material speaks for itself.

Meeting Dupont

The Dupont archive is entirely separate from the workings of the company, which is based in downtown Wilmington, not at the Hagley site. At Hagley, the division between past and present, history and ongoing business, is consciously and conscientiously maintained. And, while academic researchers are welcome at Hagley, they are generally regarded with reservation by the main corpora-tion, unless they are among the many scientific researchers that Dupont itself employs. Investigative journalists are especially disliked, but in Dupont's textile division, there is one journalistic exception – fashion editors. Fashion editors have long played a key part in the popularizing of Dupont textiles, and it was more as a fashion editor than as an anthropologist that I was able to engage with Dupont in the present. Fashion editors who are placed on the press lists of cosmetic, fashion, accessory and textile companies become an important link between producer and consumer. They are invited to company product launches, previews and briefings, and are regularly sent press releases, updates and product samples. The articles fashion editors and writers prepare for newspapers, magazines, television, websites and blogs are seen as performing an important service for consumers and producers alike – 'features' are con-sidered by consumers to be more 'authentic' and 'honest' than advertisements – and producers seek and value editors' opinions on consumer trends. Fortu-nately, my approach to Dupont coincided with a moment of corporate reflec-tion. Dupont had realized that the Boomer market existed and was expanding rapidly, and also realized they knew little about it. As one Dupont executive explained to me:

> What Dupont is interested in is the midlife shift in aspirations. The shift from a sedentary retirement to a more active period of time which may be a significant period of their total life. This coincides with seeing an active retirement as a stepping stone to a richer life, and we are inter-ested in the role of clothing in enhancing this.

They also wanted to know how Lycra affected the lives of Boomer midlifers, and what role Lycra played in this group. What drove these people, and how would this manifest in lifestyle and clothing choices? How could Dupont reach this group – through sponsorship, concerts, the traditional print and magazine media or some other means? But, at the same time, it was clear that there was a corporate ambivalence about being associated with an older group, and of being perceived as an 'old' product. As another Dupont executive told me: 'Lycra is coming up to its 40th birthday but we are playing it down.' I would remember this in time to come, but for now its significance passed me by. I was added to the Lycra press list, and agreed to share my findings about the Boomers with Dupont which, it seemed to me, would be a win–win situation, with Dupont increasing their market and hopefully the Boomers getting their leggings.

The Multi-Site Method and the Study of 'Immaterial' Culture

By the time I had been through the preliminary stages described above, a fieldwork method had become established that would prove perfect for my purposes. For some time, there had been a movement to expand anthropology's methods and interests. As MacLennan (1995: 72) put it: 'If anthropologists continue to produce primarily single-site synchronic studies and avoid vertically integrated, historical studies of power, little will be accomplished' (and see Kammen 1987: 22). 'Multi-sited ethnography' was a perfect vehicle for the anthropological study of complexity and the capitalist world system (Marcus 1995, 1998). 'Multi-site' does not mean simply carrying out fieldwork in more than one locale. Ideally, it entails a more profound pursuit of the object through time and space, in search of unexpected juxtapositions that produce new insights, and adopting the perspectives of different participants and groups along the way. This can easily become the fieldwork equivalent of a herd of wild horses, galloping off in all directions at once, and the challenge is to maintain analytic focus while going with the flow. One way of doing this – ideally suited to the anthropology of stuff – is literally, as Marcus said, to 'follow the thing', in this case, Lycra. But my research was going to be fundamentally different in one important regard. It would also be following something that wasn't there – a new approach to material culture. For, if stuff has much to tell us about society and ourselves, surely stuff that isn't there, and why, has just as much to say, if not more.

2

DUPONT

Culture, Kinship and Myth

The Brandywine winds through an American east coast landscape immortalized by the nation's greatest narrative artists including Howard Pyle and N.C. Wyeth,[1] a panorama of trees with branches like bleached bones against a pale sky, weathered barns and rocky fields where Indian corn once grew. Only sixty miles long, this river has nonetheless cut deep into the bedrock of American history and culture, for its steep descent before it emerges into Delaware Bay at Wilmington generated the power that fueled the growth of early American industry from colonial times onwards. The American flour- and corn-milling and paper-making industries began here, alongside the first American cotton-spinning factory. And, in a deep willow-shaded gorge carved by the river from blue Brandywine granite at a place now called Hagley, the quality American gunpowder industry began in 1802, as a family business that first made the Dupont name famous, and which later expanded into a diversified corporation that created much of the stuff of American life throughout the twentieth century.

From the time an American gets up in the morning until he goes to bed at night, he pays tribute to Dupont. His tooth brush is made of du Pont Nylon. The plastic cup with which he rinses his mouth is made of du Pont plastic. As he gets dressed, Dupont contributes its bit too: his suit is Dacron and wool; his wife's girdle is made with the new Lycra and so is her brassiere, and the sweater she wears with her skirt is made of Orlon. He smokes a cigarette while he's dressing, tearing the Cellophane wrapping off the pack. He peers out the window to see how the weather is and he notices in passing that the lawn looks good. It's been planted with du Pont grass seed and nourished with du Pont turf food, while the du Pont crab-grass killer got rid of that nuisance. The house has been freshly painted – inside with Lucite, outside with Dulux. And so it goes on all day. His golf balls are covered with Neoprene HC. He buys shotgun shells made by du Pont – Remington is a subsidiary – for the weekend skeet-shooting. The gasoline in his car contains an anti-knock additive made by du Pont; the brake fluid is du Pont's and so is the wax as well as the paint it covers, plus many other features of the auto. His dentist uses du Pont X-ray film. And so on – and on – and on.

(Carr 1965: 4)

Even on into outer space, where twenty of the twenty-one layers in astronaut Neil Armstrong's spacesuit were made of Dupont materials, as was the nylon flag he planted on the moon. Today Dupont continues to be omnipresent on a global scale, through a range of new products that includes pharmaceuticals and advanced electronic materials, while Lycra itself is no longer restricted to women's underwear.

How did this particular corporation, which began as a family firm, come to have such an enormous influence through inventing so much of what became the stuff of everyday American life in the twentieth century?

Until recently, capitalism 'at home' from an emic perspective has been the anthropological 'elephant in the room' of the world's most advanced capitalist nation, largely ignored by the discipline. As long ago as the 1960s, anthropologists intent on reinventing the field argued that instead of remaining 'a defensive source of knowledge about the exploited of the world rather than those who exploit them' (Hymes 1972: 51), anthropologists should study the dominant as well as the dominated, an approach that Laura Nader called 'studying up':

> If we look at the literature based on field work in the United States, we find a relatively abundant literature on the poor, the ethnic groups, the disadvantaged, there is comparatively little field research on the middle class and very little first hand work on the upper class.... What if, in reinventing anthropology, anthropologists were able to study the colonizers rather than the colonized, the culture of power rather than the culture of powerlessness, the culture of affluence rather than the culture of poverty?... The consequences of not studying up as well as down are serious in terms of developing adequate theory and description.
>
> (Nader 1972: 289–290)

Thirty years later, Nader (1997) noted that there had still been little progress in studying up at home, a gap this study aims to address.

The reluctance of academic anthropologists to engage with capitalism and corporations at home did not stop other disciplines – notably sociology – from borrowing anthropology's tools and terminology. Beginning in the 1950s, when books of popularized social science regularly made the bestseller list of the *New York Times*, writers like Vance Packard, author of *The Status Seekers* and

The Hidden Persuaders, fascinated readers with his accounts of ritualized competition in the corporate jungle and the 'savage' rivalries of status display in the suburbs, while in a more lighthearted vein, Martin Page's *The Yam Factor* compared the hierarchical organization of Wall Street executives to that of New Guinea tribes people whose place in the pecking order is determined by their wealth in yams. The alternative to these were what Koehn has called 'supply-side studies', which concentrated on the internal workings of the company rather than on its products or the larger social contexts in which the company operates, and 'demand-side business school biographies' (Koehn 2001), which focused on the careers of individual entrepreneurs within their lifetimes, giving little insight into family companies over time.

Finally, in the 1980s, business competition from abroad – primarily Japan – gave anthropologists a new incentive to study corporate capitalism at home. In a study commissioned to redress the decline in American productivity in the face of foreign competition, sociologists Deal and Kennedy concluded that management techniques alone could not explain the success of some companies and products, and the failure of others. Instead, they found that successful companies were distinguished by a strong 'corporate culture, a cohesion of values, myths, heroes and symbols that has come to mean a great deal to the people who work there' (Deal and Kennedy 1982: 4–5). In a survey of eighty large American and foreign companies, Deal and Kennedy identified eighteen commercially successful 'strong culture companies', of which Dupont was one of the strongest. Few systematic details of the cultures were given, but of the eighteen – Caterpillar Tractor, General Electric, DuPont, Chubb Insurance, Price Waterhouse & Co, Jefferson-Smurfit, Digital Equipment Corporation, Proctor & Gamble, Hewlett-Packard, Leo Burnett Advertising Agency, Johnson & Johnson, Tandem Computer, Continental Bank, 3M, The Training Services Administration Agency of the British Government, International Business Machines (IBM), Dana Corporation and the Rouse Company – the first twelve had begun as family firms, or were still being, or had recently been, operated by their founders at the time of the study.

Values, myths, symbols, heroes and family/kinship are familiar anthropological territory, but the anthropological study of large and long-established family firms has fallen victim to the current anthropological bias against elites. Although a colorful procession of leopard-skin chiefs, sacred kings, high chieftesses, jaguar priests, war leaders, headmen, royal priestesses and many more pass through the anthropological classics, as a result of the relentless studying down of recent times, there has so far been only one full-scale anthropological study of elite American business families. *Lives In Trust* (1992), by anthropologist George Marcus with historian Peter Dobkin Hall, examines a number of dynastic American families grown wealthy on business, including the Rockefellers (Standard Oil), the Gettys (Getty Oil) and the Hunts (Hunt Oil Company), focusing on two lesser-known Texas families, the Kempners and the Moodys, also enriched by oil. This study examined the way family dynasties are perpetuated through fiduciary trusts rather than family businesses as such, and it was not until 2002 that Yanagisako's *Producing Culture and Capital* showed what anthropology can bring to the study of capitalism that is both different to, and as valuable as, conventional studies in economic and business history.[2]

In this work, Yanagisako combined ethnography with theory and archival research to show how kinship dynamics and associated origin myths, family narratives and cultural values influenced the conduct of business among family firms of silk producers in Como, Italy. This unusual approach – complex and challenging for those accustomed to 'pure' business or 'pure' anthropological studies, or to working on just one level of analysis – produced unique emic insights into the dynamics of family businesses. However, the firms in question were relatively small and not geared to mass production, and Yanagisako's study did not extend to stuff – the products made by the firms – or to culture in the wider sense of attitudes and values that might influence the producers and the products, or the interaction between producers and consumers. Building on her work, I decided to use Lycra and Dupont as the focus of in-depth anthropological study of whether, and how, family traits and values, symbols, ritual and myth can become embedded in practices and organizations, finally emerging in material form as distinctive mass-market products formed by family values – products that could influence society and economy on a wide scale.

The search for answers begins with what anthropologists call 'origin myths'. Origin myths – the 'story people tell themselves about themselves' (Geertz 1973) – are primary cultural texts that anthropologists seek out in other societies, recognizing as Malinowski first noted that

> an intimate connection exists between the word, *mythos*, the sacred tales of a tribe on the one hand, and their ritual acts, their moral deeds, their social organization, and even their practical activities, on the other.
>
> (Yanagisako and Delaney 1994: 2)

In their own societies, however, anthropologists tend to ignore origin myths, particularly 'official' origin myths, dismissing them as superstition, invention or hagiography. This goes against cultural common sense. Family narratives, both official and unofficial, are full of mythic significance, and are also often contesting accounts of the historic past. As such, they are a rich resource for investigating the interaction between culture, capitalism, kinship and stuff over time.

Hagley, a 168-acre estate three miles outside Wilmington, Delaware, was the site of the first Dupont business enterprise, where the DuPont family lived and worked for generations in buildings that are still standing, and where the DuPont family cemetery – still in use – is located. Hagley is where the Dupont archive is held, but it is much more than a research and heritage center, for it is comprised of elements – ancestral houses, the family burying place, a landscape shaped by preceding generations, a palpable sense of ancestor veneration – that anthropologists would instantly recognize as making Hagley sacred ground if met with in another society. Encountered at home, the anthropologist has two choices: to reject the notion that this is a mythic landscape full of meanings, or to be drawn into it, its narratives and its myths, and I chose the latter.

Anthropologists know that the two most important things about myths are: first, what matters about a myth is not whether it is true, but whether it is *believed* to be true; second, there is likely to be more than one myth about any one place, person, event or thing. What matters is not which version is 'right', but what the differences between them tell us. With Dupont, as Yanagisako found with her Como firms, there were three levels of origin myth: the official history of the founding of the firm, alternative accounts of the founding of the firm and stories about 'before the firm was founded'. In their different ways, each demonstrates that 'in a corporation, a creation story is not a neutral thing, it helps to shape policy, at least tacitly if not overtly' (Hounshell 1990: 407; see also Holt 2004). The narrative may be uneven, veering in the case of Dupont from something very like a fairytale through moral fable, historical narrative, company hagiography, family history and back again, but it is nonetheless deeply revealing of family and firm. All three levels of myth are essential to understand the complexity of the family heritage that influenced the firm and its products.

Of these myths, the official history always seems to be the most straightforward. Invariably, it celebrates the founder, and is essentially an affirmation of the company as it is now. There are no nuances, no suggestion that things might have turned out otherwise, and the path to success is presented as inevitable. Official histories tend to be corporate 'just so' stories, edited versions of the past that justify the way things are in the present. This is not to say that official narratives are without value; quite the reverse. But this can only be appreciated by comparing them to other versions of the myth, and a common mistake made by those who discount the importance of company narratives is that they have often looked only at this kind of myth.

The Official Narrative of the Founding of the Firm

The official history of the founding of Dupont is *Du Pont: The Autobiography of an American Enterprise*, published privately by Dupont in 1952 to mark the one-hundred-and-fiftieth anniversary of the company. It was not intended for a wide public audience, but was expressly written for 'employees, retirees and the general public', in that order. The *Autobiography* is a paradigm of popular American narrative history seen through the lens of capitalist enterprise. It is also a significant social document of the period in which it was written – a time when the belief in progress was strong and big business was perceived as heroic, when science was valorized and when national identity was a source of unmixed pride. It is a work of public culture – the way Dupont wished to be seen – that reflects a private culture, the way Dupont, family and company, saw itself.

There are three features that distinguish the *Autobiography* from standard company histories. First, it is history as told through stuff – history presented through inventions, industry, popular culture and specific products, in the context of social change. Second, it specifically highlights the importance of workers, both as producers and as consumers, with the founder and sub-sequent generations of the DuPont family presented as *primus inter pares* – first among equals – workers themselves, in pursuit with their employees of the common goals of progress and betterment. It also emphasizes the importance the company always gave to fulfilling the needs of the *mass* market. Third, the work explicitly identifies Dupont, company and family, with the nation, as seen in this paragraph with which the book begins:

This is a book without an author, just as it is a story without an end.... Du Pont grew because the growing nation's needs and its free traditions encouraged progress. The nation grew because Du Pont, and a thousand others, were contributing the seeds of growth that germinate in daring, risk and innovation. Generations of men and women played their parts in this development, from a single powder mill to a company national in scope and significance. Over the years they have shared heartbreaks and despair, as well as the satisfactions and rewards. But the company that has emerged rests, like the nation, on a base finely tempered in the fires of time. It is a story set down over the years, written into the record by the lives of the thousands who participated, as day follows day. This is their story, as they themselves have enacted it: the autobiography of an American enterprise.

(Dupont 1952:1)

The official account of the company's foundation given in the *Autobiography* is as follows. Eleuthère Irénée du Pont, known as Irénée, arrived in America from France on New Year's Day 1800, in the company of his elder brother Victor and their 'distinguished' father Pierre Samuel du Pont, 'a career man in government service … who had been raised to the nobility for helping to

Figure 2.1 Portrait of Irénée Dupont by Rembrandt Peale, courtesy of Hagley Museum and Library.

effect the Peace of Paris between England and the United States in 1782'
(Dupont 1952: 6).

The twenty-eight-year-old Irénée, described as 'scientifically inclined', had
been apprenticed to 'the famed French chemist Antoine Lavoisier, the greatest scientist of his day, superintendent of the government gunpowder plant at
Essone ... [where he] learned the craft of powdermaking and acquired a
precise sense of the scientific method' (Dupont 1952: 8). The aristocratic
Lavoisier fell victim to the Revolution and the guillotine, after Maximilien
Robespierre – driving force behind the Reign of Terror – declared that France
had no need of scientists. The Duponts left France shortly afterwards.

According to the *Autobiography*, Irénée's original intention, with his father
and elder brother, was to 'set up a sort of colony in which Frenchmen like
himself could start life anew'. The colony would 'contain farms, sawmills to
provide lumber for homes and barns, factories to make glassware and pottery,
and a suitable compliment of schools, churches and stores' (Dupont 1952:
11). The colony was to be financed through venture capital, but sufficient
funds were not forthcoming and the family's future was uncertain when
Irénée, out on a day's hunting, made his first purchase of American gunpowder and found it to be far inferior to the French powder that Lavoisier had
taught him to make. He also realized that good powder was a necessity in the
new nation, not only for shooting game but for protection, and for clearing
land for agriculture and roads. 'Here was an opportunity of the sort businesses
are built on: a human need waiting for someone with the skill and enterprise
to see that it is filled' (DuPont 1952: 10). Irénée raised capital by selling shares
in the newly formed E.I. du Pont de Nemours & Company, purchased powder-
making machinery in France, selected the Hagley site on the Brandywine and
began constructing a powder works there in July 1802. The first Dupont
powder went on public sale in 1804, and by 1811 the Dupont powder mills
were the largest in America, with the quality of Dupont powder reckoned to
be the best in the nation.

The *Autobiography* presents Irénée as the ideal anthropological ancestor,
hero and founder, a visionary who uses his personal abilities to found his firm,
establish his family and create his own destiny. As Yanagisako observes, 'Fathering a family and fathering a business are mutually interdependent projects of
creation in this cosmology of kinship and business, family and capitalism'
(Yanagisako 2002: 69). The success of the company is attributed directly to
Irénée, who insisted that 'quality was a matter of pride with which no compro-
mise could be made' (Dupont 1952: 19). He also, we are told,

constantly sought means to increase the quality of his product and
improve his methods – the familiar product-and-process improvement

approach of present day industry. He even, it is claimed, anticipated the modern device of enlarging a company's income and usefulness by what is now called 'diversification.'

(Dupont 1952: 21)

He did this by pioneering the use and sale of the by-products of powder-making.

The Alternative Narrative of the Founding of the Firm

The alternative narrative of the founding of the firm is embedded in the very landscape of Hagley. The estate, which describes itself as 'an open air museum on the site of the birthplace of the DuPont Company' is today a place of bucolic tranquility and reverential silence where the past may be contemplated with the respect it deserves. Dupont family members still live there, protected from prying eyes by high hedges and locked gates. Tour visitors are closely supervised and taken around by minibus, even for short distances, while staff and researchers who stay overnight on the site must stick to the few marked paths that cross the estate. This is no historical theme park built for amusement; Hagley does not seek to trivialize the past it celebrates. Its declared purpose is not to entertain but to educate, to 'tell the story of the du Ponts and their workers as part of the broader history of industry and technology in America', as the Hagley brochure puts it. However, as with the official narrative of the *Autobiography*, the story the Hagley site tells is initially only partial.

To visit Hagley today is to step into a living lithographic print by Currier and Ives, in which a rural landscape has been given the appearance of an idyllic country park, hand-colored in harmonious and genteel pastel shades. The banks of the Brandywine, the waters of which now run limpid and clear, are home to ornamental ducks and geese. Squirrels gambol on grassy hillsides, darting between the stands of trees that seem to have been there from time immemorial. There are no human figures to be seen, and the few immaculately kept buildings that intrude upon the sweeping vistas appear at first to have been designed as ornamental follies. They are, however, original working buildings.

Dupont powder was processed in the low stone sheds of Brandywine granite that crouch sphinx-like in pairs along the creek. Nearby stand the rolling mill, the press house, the steam-engine house and the wheelwright's shop, all with restored antique equipment and attendants, often retired employees, anxious to demonstrate the machines and explain their workings. The road through the estate continues on past the Sunday School where the workers' children learned to read and write, taught by the DuPont daughters, then curves up to the knoll where the first DuPont family house overlooks the park and creek. The house itself is unpretentious and simply furnished, a dwelling in the early Federalist style notable only for the profusion of American eagle ornaments. Two small stone buildings flank the main house. On the left is the First Office, the single-room structure from where the company was run for over a century, with successive family members using Irénée's original chair and desk, following his example of personally controlling every aspect of the running of the company, partly wearing away the floor beneath his chair and desk in the process. On the right is the First Workshop, where three generations of the family experimented with chemicals and machinery. A DuPont might work on a process or formula, put his notes aside, and have another family member carry on the work, even one or two generations later. The placement of the buildings are Levi-Straussian (1963) in their symbolism: the source of wealth to one side, the place where the wealth was managed to the other, and the house, symbolizing the family, in between.

In the end, the visitor to Hagley is left with some understanding of the powder-making process, an appreciation of the work involved, an acquaintance with the way the first DuPonts and their workers lived – and more questions than answers. How did this Arcadian landscape produce gunpowder on an industrial scale? And how did this sleepy rural enclave devoted to producing a single product spawn a transnational diversified corporation? The most recent official history, issued in 2002 to mark the bicentenary of the company's founding, is not illuminating. The company succeeded, it suggests, because 'it observed strict standards, used the latest technology and production methods and practiced sound management' (Kinnane 2002: 16), but this cannot be the whole story. The answer to the first question can be seen in a print I found of Hagley dating from 1854. The site is barely recognizable, dominated by closely built structures that were razed long ago. Black smoke pours from tall chimneys, the space between buildings is crisscrossed with tracks made by the wagons that hauled powder around the estate and out to customers, and workers swarm everywhere like ants. It is as industrial a scene as any in the north of England in the same period. Neither somnolent nor pretty, *this* was the landscape that produced the powder – but what produced and drove the du Pont family?

In alternate accounts of the foundation of a family firm, a more kinship-oriented narrative and a wider cast of characters emerges. The single heroic figure is joined by siblings and other relatives who co-founded the firm or worked in it, by business partnerships formalized through marriage, and by women relatives. Disputes between siblings and cousins over the succession, personal disagreements that altered the conduct of the firm and business partnerships that ended acrimoniously, common to all family firms, come to light. The alternative account is also the site of the working out of moral issues that justify or challenge the official account, for this kind of narrative is often used by the 'inner circle' to justify their position through reference to the past. It is also used by those in the 'outer circle' who seek to use the past to change or clarify their own present status. Facts emerge – like debts and other difficulties – that show the path to progress presented in the official account was not as quick or easy as it is made to seem. The Dupont alternative narrative uses the different characters and interests of the two Dupont immigrant brothers to justify the relative degree of involvement of their descendants in the firm, and also suggests that the relationship between the young Irénée and the childless Lavoisiers may have been closer than that of mentor and student, implying informal adoption,[3] further justifying the company's mythic and mystical 'ownership' of chemistry.

The Narrative of Before the Firm Was Founded

Focusing on the period that preceded the foundation, this kind of narrative differs markedly from both the official and alternate accounts because it throws light on prior factors that may have influenced the foundation and operation of the firm. Examining archival sources in a variety of repositories including the *Bibliothèque Nationale* in Paris, it quickly becomes apparent that to the family itself, the ancestral figure of the Dupont origin myth is not Irénée, but his father Pierre Samuel, known within the family as 'Bon Papa'. In its telling, the story shifts from a near-fairytale to moral fable, narrative history, politico-economic tract and back again. The only primary source for the earliest stages of the myth is the fragmentary autobiography of Pierre Samuel du Pont, compiled and published privately by his descendants along with many of his other personal papers, as part of what the translator of the patriarch's memoir has called 'the veritable cult they constructed around his memory' (Dupont 1984: 3). This filial and mythologizing project has continued, with later generations memorializing the writings and achievements of their predecessors, down to the present. Written in 1792, some forty years after the events it describes, the patriarch's autobiography takes the form of letters to his two sons. In it, the Protestant paternal Dupont line, consisting of artisans, peasants and small traders, is quickly dismissed, apart from noting that they are the source of the distinctive and prominent 'Dupont nose', the phenotypic or visual outward sign of Dupont family descent. This interest in phenotype and genotype (invisible genetic inheritance), at the very heart of kinship beliefs universally, was captured in the 1917 poem *Heredity* by Thomas Hardy:

I am the Family Face
Flesh perishes, I live on,
Projecting trait and trace
Through time to times anon.
And leaping from place to place
Over oblivion.

The maternal de Montchanin line, by contrast, receives a great deal of attention. The de Montchanins were of noble antecedents but had fallen on hard times, and had been 'derogated' or dropped from the aristocracy because they had been forced to earn a living through trade. Nonetheless, the mother of the future patriarch had been raised as a noblewoman in the house of a marquis, a distant de Montchanin relation, as a companion to the marquis's daughter. There she was well educated, and also grew into a beauty, contributing another feature to the 'family face'. As the patriarch wrote to his sons: 'The dimple that decorated her chin has passed to you, and I like to think that you will transmit it to your children' (Dupont 1984: 104). Sent away from the marquis's house when she came of age because she was not a social equal, the girl who had been raised 'like a princess' and now possessing nothing in the world, married a Parisian clockmaker called Samuel Dupont and became a clockmaker herself, 'humiliated without daring to admit it, by being reduced to work with her hands in order to live' (Dupont 1984: 118), her son wrote. In her reduced circumstances, Anne de Montchanin retained the manners and attitudes of the aristocracy, telling her eldest son Pierre Samuel stories of men who rose from humble beginnings to win ennoblement, and passing her educational accomplishments on to him, which her husband opposed. As his son recalled:

In his view, a trade could provide the only good guarantee of peace and subsistence. He was not entirely wrong, but I had to spend fifty years and successively put my finger on all the keys of life to return to his opinion, which my mother never shared. . . . My father did not want his children to rise above his station.

(Dupont 1984: 123; original italics)

Anne de Montchanin died when Pierre Samuel was ten. After struggling for a further ten years to combine clock-making with studying, he broke away from his father and eventually managed to join the circle surrounding the extraordinary group known as the Encyclopaedists, creators of the *Encyclopédie, ou dictionnaire raisonné des sciences, des arts et des métiers*, a key text of the Enlightenment, whose members included the essayist and philosopher Denis Diderot (1713–1784) and the mathematician, physicist and philosopher Jean d'Alembert (1719–1783), thus gaining entry to the leading intellectual and political circles of the last days of the *Ancien Régime*. From now onwards, Pierre Samuel's account is corroborated by independent contemporary records in France, Britain and America. Pierre Samuel became secretary to François Quesnay (1694–1774), whom he described as a 'second father' at a time when Quesnay was devising a new theory of political economy – the first complete system of economics – based on the belief that free trade, resulting in increased profits, and the accumulation of capital and surplus was the way to simultaneously increase wealth, the power of the state and the well-being of its people, for whom the landlords had a paternalistic responsibility. These views ultimately influenced Adam Smith and Karl Marx. Pierre Samuel gave the theory the name by which it became known – Physiocracy – and claimed to have independently arrived at the same conclusions as Quesnay. Under Quesnay's patronage, Pierre Samuel moved on to work for Turgot (Anne Robert Jacques Turgot, Baron de Laune, 1727–1781, an early advocate of economic liberalism), one of the reforming ministers of the *Ancien Régime*, before writing a book entitled *Physiocracy, or the Natural Constitution of that Form of Government Most Advantageous to the Human Race*. The book attracted the attention of American statesman and scientist Benjamin Franklin, then on a visit to France, who became a valued friend. Pierre Samuel also formed a close friendship with Antoine Laurent Lavoisier, the father of modern chemistry. Under King Louis XVI, Pierre Samuel helped to negotiate the Treaty of Paris by which Britain recognized the independence of her former American colonies, thus coming to the notice of Thomas Jefferson, the future third President of the United States, who also became a friend. In recognition of his success in the treaty negotiations, Pierre Samuel was awarded a royal patent of nobility, making him a *chevalier* and entitling him to add the aristocratic prefix 'de' to his surname. He now became known as Pierre Samuel du Pont de Nemours, Nemours being the district where he purchased a country estate with money lent to him by Lavoisier.

With tremendous effort, Pierre Samuel had managed to raise himself to the nobility, thus fulfilling his mother's hopes. He had attained a position of prominence that allowed him to promote his physiocratic views, and to pursue personal financial security. Along the way he had married, later becoming a widower with two sons for whom he had arranged what seemed to be settled futures. Now, at the pinnacle of success, he suffered the supreme irony of seeing everything he had hoped and worked for swept away when the Revolution broke out. Born a man of the people, he was now perceived by the mob as a hereditary class enemy, and became an object of their wrath. As the Reign of Terror ran its course, many of Pierre Samuel's friends lost their lives on the scaffold. Seen as too liberal by the royalists and too moderate by the extremists, Pierre Samuel was incarcerated in the notorious La Force prison and sentenced to death, saved from the guillotine only by the timely murder of Robespierre.

The Road to Pontiana

Seeing no future for himself or his sons in France, Pierre Samuel devised a grand scheme to emigrate to America, and establish an agricultural colony organized in accordance with physiocratic principles, to be financed by venture capital. The colony, envisioned more on the scale of a small state than a settlement, would be self-sufficient and was expected to produce profits for its investors. Ultimately, Pierre Samuel intended that the colony – to be called Pontiana – would be part of an extensive trading network linking America with Europe. At the time, similar projects were being contemplated by other entrepreneurs who wanted to establish their own trading empires or even independent states in the regions of the North American continent which had not yet been claimed by Europeans. One such was John Jacob Astor, who planned to found 'Astoria', a trans-Pacific trading empire located on the Pacific Northwest Coast in the present-day state of Oregon, where a coastal city bears the name of the empire that never was.[4]

Although investors in Pontiana included the noted diplomat Talleyrand, General the Marquis de Lafayette, hero of the American War of Independence, and the philosopher Jean-Jacques Rousseau, sufficient funding was not forthcoming and in the end Pierre Samuel, his sons and their wives and children sailed from France to an uncertain future on a ship called the *American Eagle*, arriving in America on the last day of 1799. In America, anti-French sentiment was running high in reaction to the excesses of the Terror, and because of rumors that the French were planning to extend their possessions in North America. Franklin was dead, and Jefferson, whose political party was out of power, could do little to help them. Living on capital, the DuPonts soon found themselves in financial difficulties, and their situation was becoming desperate when Irénée spotted a gap in the American gunpowder market. But it was Pierre Samuel, despite the fact that he strongly disapproved of the family entering a low-status trade, who facilitated the project by soliciting Jefferson for future American government orders for Dupont powder even before the mills had been built, following it up with Jefferson, who by now had been elected America's third President, as soon as the first powder was ready. This began the Dupont Company's close association with the American government, which continues to this day. While Irénée had the technical knowledge and professional dedication, it was Pierre Samuel's socioeconomic vision and political contacts that shaped the company's future.

The early years of the Dupont powderworks also saw the establishment of a distinctive way of life for the family. Every aspect of the mill's construction and

operation was based on methods learned from Lavoisier, a heritage perpetuated in company ritual today through the Lavoisier Medal given to outstand-
ing scientists in the company's employ, and the Lavoisier Academy, the
company's own scientific hall of fame. The extended Dupont family and their
workers became a colony in miniature, physically and socially isolated on the
Hagley site, in effect remaining a closed group for three generations. The
physical isolation was necessary in order to conceal the secrets of their French
powder manufacturing methods, and for safety because of the ever-present
danger of explosions. The reasons for their social isolation were more
complex.

The Duponts practiced a kind of family communism. No family member,
including the founder Irénée, owned property as individuals. The houses they
lived in and the horses they rode, as well as the mills, the land and the food they
ate, all belonged to the company. No family members received a salary, but drew
from company funds according to their needs. Male Duponts had to start at the
bottom in the powder mills and work their way up, subsequently finding employment in a branch of the business best suited to them, but knowing how the
company as a whole worked. Dupont females could inherit shares in the business but their formal involvement was limited to acting as sleeping (non-active)
partners in the company. On the informal level, the day-to-day efforts of all
Dupont women supported the family enterprise within the home, and through
their involvement with the welfare of the workers and their families (see Catanese 1997). The life of the business was inseparable from that of the family.

This is a paradigm example of how myth and anthropological methods can
throw new light upon capitalist processes. The family communism and physiocracy are not part of the official Dupont narrative and are glossed over in the
other accounts; supplementary family papers and other sources have been
drawn upon here. As a reflection of this official invisibility, they have not
figured in academic works on Dupont's history or operations where Dupont is
treated like any other corporation, and assumed to be motivated solely by
'profit' achieved through conventional practice. The anthropological analysis
of myth and family tradition paints a very different picture, and raises questions that are central to political/economic analysis. What are the connections
between the early economic ideology of physiocracy – with its incipient
notions of self-regulation, strong property rights, individual work ethic and
laissez-faire ideals – the founding of capitalism in general, and the development of the formative ideas and values of the United States in particular? How
did the Duponts promote physiological ideals through their links with the
founding fathers?[5] Outside the scope of this study, questions like these demonstrate the benefits of what Sahlins called 'an economics properly anthropological', and the benefits of a holistic case study.

The Dupont family's social isolation was further increased by the high incidence of cousin marriage among them. This was the form of alliance that Pierre Samuel had favored for his colony of Pontiana: 'The marriages that I should prefer for our colony would be between the cousins. In that way we should be sure of honesty of soul and purity of blood' (Pierre Samuel DuPont, in Carr 1965: 127).

The practice of marrying cousins continued over several generations, enhanced by sibling marriages (two members of the Dupont family marrying two members of another family) and partnership marriages (business partnerships consolidated through marriage). In the eighteenth and nineteenth centuries, cousin marriages were a common way of forging and maintaining political links, economic ties and circles of social influence that led to the rise of the bourgeois generally, and to the success of family dynasties like the Wedgwoods and the Rothschilds (Kuper 2001), but no family practiced it on the scale of the Duponts. This effectively distanced the Duponts from the wider community, and led to deep suspicion of the family among outsiders, exacerbated by the fact that, in this nation of immigrants, the family were seen as 'foreign' because of their French descent.

The children of these marriages developed their own *patois*, full of family references which outsiders found it impossible to understand, and when they grew up to take their places in the business, the men often referred to each other simply as 'Brother' and to themselves in the third person, often beginning business letters written by themselves with 'Our Mr. Alfred' or 'Our Mr. Henry'. One of the consequences of these cousin marriages was the duplication and repetition among males of first names taken from the members of the founding generation – Alfred Victor, Alfred Irénée, Alexis Irénée, Eleuthère Irénée Sr. and Jr., Irénée Sr. and Jr., Lammot I–III, Pierre Samuel I–IV and Henry I–V among them. Female names were also passed down, and sometimes the male names were feminized, as in 'Irene'. The significance of naming practices of this kind is well-known in anthropology. As Bourdieu (1977: 36) put it:

> Names … are emblems, symbolizing the whole symbolic capital accumulated by a lineage … it gives those who are in a dominant position the opportunity to profess the veneration of the past which is best suited to legitimate their present interests. To give a new-born child the name of a great forefather is not simply to perform an act of filial piety, but also in a sense to predestine the child thus named to bring the eponymous ancestor 'back to life', i.e. to succeed him in his responsibilities and his powers.

Among the Duponts, cousin marriage supported by sibling and partnership marriage counteracted the centrifugal tendencies that split families that 'marry out'. They also consolidated the lineage and clarified politico-jural issues of family succession and corporate continuity, which in any case the system of family communism also held in check. Neither the family commun- ism nor the cousin marriages are mentioned in the two official histories of the firm, illustrating the importance of examining all forms of family myth in order to construct a full picture of the internal dynamics of family and firm.

The paternalism practiced within the Dupont clan was extended to their employees, with whom the family, and later the company, sought to develop and foster a labor system in which the mutual interests of employer and employees were seen as inseparably linked: 'by cooperating in the effort to achieve a common goal – the continuing expansion of the Du Pont Company's production – managers and workers together would reap the benefits of prosperity' (Rumm 1989: vii). Labor relations as such are outside the scope of this study. What is important here is that this is the emic view, the way the Dupont family saw relations with their workers from the early days onwards, and the roots of that emic view. This 'mutuality' was subject to ongoing negotiation, with the employees receiving better pay and benefits, and the employers better work and more stability of employment over time. 'Fair dealings' cutting both ways were considered a core company and family value. At least one senior member of the family was always on hand in the yards at Hagley, superintending operations, while young Dupont males worked alongside the workers, learning each stage of the powder-making operation, and all those Duponts active in the management of the company spent as much time as possible in the yards laboring with the employees. Like the DuPont family, their employees 'worked, played, married and were buried within the geographical confines of the Du Pont property' (Chandler and Salisbury 1971: 5), many families working for the DuPonts for genera- tions. For employees, as for the DuPonts, the company was not just a place to work, it was a way of life.

Bound by ties of blood, marriage and employment intensified by physical and social isolation, living and dying within sound of the powder works, the Duponts developed a strong attachment to and identification with the land on the Brandywine. It was the original source of their wealth, their birthplace, a site of continuing inspiration and the place where they would one day be laid to rest in the family cemetery, in the middle of which lay the old patriarch Pierre Samuel, who died at the age of seventy-eight after helping to put out a fire in the powder works. Duponts were buried to the patriarch's right if they descended from the elder son Victor, and to his left if descended from Irénée. Much of this is apparent in the decorative map of the property commissioned by the family from Brandywine artist Frank Schoonover, and drawn by him using family records and oral reminiscences.

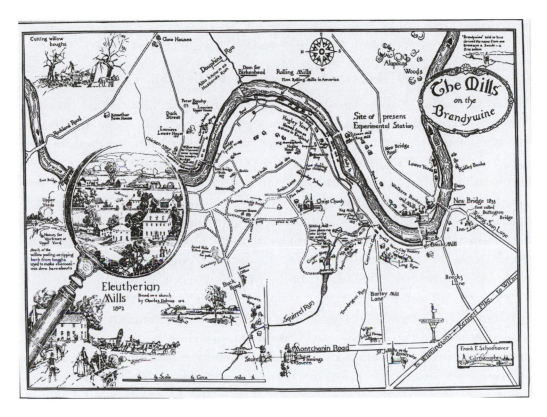

Figure 2.2 Map of Hagley by Frank Schoonover, courtesy of Hagley Museum and Library.

Here the mythic and physical landscapes, the past and the present, fuse in a visualization of collective memory, a portrayal of the way the family saw itself and the land. Long-vanished features are shown next to existing ones, their prominence reflecting a significance known to the family but not to outsiders, while captions like 'keg mill' and 'slitting mill' sit next to one that says 'fine sledding for children'. Dotted about the map are names like *Montchanin, Louviers* and *Nemours,* family and estate names from France dating from before the foundation of the firm and transplanted to the new world where they were bestowed on mansions in the chateau style built by later generations of Duponts, intensifying the family's identification with the Brandywine land while at the same time linking that land to a more distant time and place. The few proper names that appear on the map are those of DuPont relatives: the Dupont name is not shown. Implicitly, everything not otherwise noted *is* Dupont.

The map was drawn for inclusion in the *Autobiography,* the official 1952 history of the firm, and also appeared in the 2002 version (Kinnane 2002). Its most striking feature, which has not been commented on before, is that on this otherwise highly detailed and historically sensitive map, the words 'gun'

and 'powder' do not appear. By the time the map was drawn, the family wished
to disassociate itself publicly from the product in which it was rooted.

From Family Business to Business Family to Public Company

This returns the analysis to what anthropologists call 'naturalized practice'
(Geertz 1973), the taken-for-granted understandings with roots in the past
which explain 'why we do things the way we do around here'. Disentangling
the three levels of Dupont origin myths produces a private narrative that is
much more rich and complex than the official public account. It is these
dynamics of kinship and the specifics of the DuPont family history – rather
than generalized organizational dynamics and management structures as business historians like Alfred D. Chandler (1972, 1978) would have it – that facilitated Dupont's transition from a single-product company to a diversified
corporation, dictated the organization of that corporation and shaped its
future methods and products.

When the first Irénée died in 1834, ownership of the company passed to his
sons and daughters in seven equal shares. Dupont then became a family partnership under the direction of a triumvirate of three senior partners, either
brothers or cousins, all descended from Irénée. Over the next sixty years,
there were three of these triumvirates, headed by Alfred Dupont I, Henry
Dupont I and then Eugene Dupont I, and the business on the Brandywine
continued to grow, run exactly as Irénée had run it, while the family itself also
continued to grow. A century after the company was founded, there was a succession crisis. The reasons were partly personal, partly structural, summed up
in the adage – 'the first generation makes it, the second develops it, the third
destroys it'. Three generations from the founder is generally the point at
which the competing demands of family members become critical. The usual
strategies employed to preserve continuity or cope with change include the
establishment of fiduciary trusts (Marcus and Hall 1992), the winding up of
the business followed by the founding of new firms run by descendants (Yanagisako 2002), or the segmentation of the family business into autonomous
branches, as with the Rothschilds (Kuper 2001). Sometimes the businesses
themselves continue, although the family loses control of them, as happened
with the American firms Armour (meatpacking) and Westinghouse (electrical
goods). In the case of the Duponts, the crisis happened in the fourth
generation.

At this point, three Dupont cousins, all of whom had married their cousins,
took control of the organization and turned it from a private family firm run
as a partnership into a public company in which the family retained a controlling interest. The policy of automatically employing family members was dis-
continued, although relatives of proven ability were encouraged to join the

firm. The three cousins – Alfred Dupont III, Pierre Samuel Dupont II and T. Coleman Dupont – relocated everything but the powder mills from the Brandywine to modern purpose-built premises in Wilmington, expanded the company and entered into a series of mergers with smaller explosives firms, ending in the formation of the Powder Trust, which effectively controlled American domestic powder sales.

Dupont's salesmen came to be regarded as the elite troops of the explosives industry. Many had formal training in chemistry, essential for understanding powder and explosives, and they were under instructions to solve the customers' problems for them, working from their own knowledge and from special Dupont manuals that gave detailed instructions for everything from removing tree stumps efficiently to storing powder safely. They were well-paid, dedicated – competitors called them ruthless – and renowned for their company loyalty and *esprit de corps.*

It was at this time that the red and white 'Du Pont Oval' was created in the company advertising department. Irénée Dupont had been against advertising, disliking 'all that savors of self praise and bragging',[6] arguing that the quality of the product and the renown of the Dupont name were sufficient to guarantee sales, and that if money was to be spent, it should be on product development, not publicity. Now, with the company expanding, it was felt that some kind of identifying and unifying trademark was needed, something that could be used on all Dupont products. First used in public in 1907, it became one of the most recognized and respected corporate logos in the world, while in private it acted as a reminder and reinforcer of Dupont's unique family heritage and company values. It was used almost subliminally on everything from company writing paper and service pins to paperweights, ashtrays, keychains and watch fobs, imbuing everything on which it appeared with a near-mystical aura. In the firm, it became known as 'Dupont's best salesman'. As the company put it:

> Du Pont's top salesman receives neither a salary nor a commission, never reports a sale and never turns in an expense account. He has no office of his own, but makes himself home in yours or mine. And while he never rings a doorbell, he gets in more homes, sees more customers and makes more sales than any regular Du Pont salesman ever could.[7]

However, having abandoned the relative anonymity of the Brandywine and having formalized trade 'understandings' that had previously been tacit, the company found itself exposed to unwelcome public attention. The American government brought a suit against Dupont on the grounds that they had violated the Sherman Antitrust Act by eliminating competition and fixing prices, thus creating a monopoly of the explosives business. The loss of the suit in 1911, after a protracted legal battle, had a profound, indeed visceral, effect upon the company. The steel, oil, railroad, telephone and meatpacking industries were all the subject of anti-trust investigations and actions on similar grounds during this period of widespread feeling against big business (Marchand 1985, 1998; Noble 1977). Dupont's reaction to the prosecution had an intensely personal dimension, since criticism of the company was also criticism of the family. Dupont immediately set out to change the way they were perceived by the public, and to transform the way they operated in private.

Dupont products had tamed the American wilderness, built American industry and supported the defense of the nation, while on the personal level the relations between the founding figures of the firm – Pierre Samuel and Irénée – and of the nation – Benjamin Franklin and Thomas Jefferson – had been close. What had always been a part of Dupont family private culture was now taken onto the public stage. The Dupont Company became a patron of popular art and a creator of public culture through its support of what came to be called the 'Brandywine School' because of its location in the Brandywine Valley. Flourishing under the direction of artist Howard Pyle between 1894 and 1911, it gave rise through his work, and after his death that of his students, to the golden age of American illustration that continued to the 1950s, when it was overwhelmed by photography. Bridging the gap between 'fine' and 'popular' art, the distinctive work of the school caught the imagination of a public who, struggling to adapt to modernity, longed for the certainties, values and traditions of the nation's historic past. Pictures of the soldiers and battles of the War of Independence, of pilgrims celebrating the first Thanksgiving, of pioneers and frontiersmen engaged in the daily life of the young republic, became icons of secular devotion, affirming and perpetuating the values and vision of the founding fathers. To the DuPont family, the development of the company had always been closely identified with that of the nation, and through their sponsorship of public culture, the nation came to see things the same way.

Artists of the Brandywine School had previously executed portraits of family members, invariably showing them with the distinctive DuPont nose and chin. The company now commissioned Brandywine artists to depict episodes from Dupont's early days, such as Howard Pyle's *Conestoga Powder Wagon* which shows a Dupont gunpowder wagon en route to supply American troops during the War of 1812, the last picture Pyle ever painted; other works included a portrait of Irénée Dupont's 1801 meeting with Thomas Jefferson and Paul Revere. The company also commissioned artwork for magazine and newspaper advertisements that identified Dupont with the American pioneering spirit and the foundations of the country itself. Generations of Americans

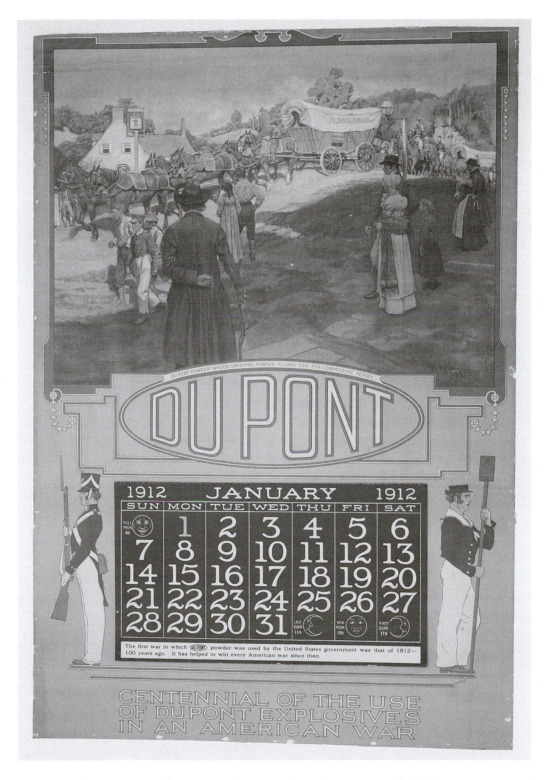

Figure 2.3 Conestoga Powder Wagon by Howard Pyle, courtesy of Hagley Museum and Library.

would grow up never realizing that the iconic pictures of the nation's past that became a central part of public culture of the period were, directly or indirectly, pictures of Dupont's past. This brilliant propaganda strategy served to promote Dupont's corporate ideology while cementing the family's image as the nation's benefactors.

Even before the monopoly lawsuit, the company had begun to seek new uses for nitrocellulose, which was used in the manufacture of smokeless powder. The terms of settlement obliged Dupont to divest itself of direct control over two-thirds of its general explosives business, although the smokeless powder facilities which had long supplied the military were allowed to remain intact on the grounds of national security. Decried in the company's official history as 'division by degree' from its birthright, some members of the family came to see the settlement as a blessing in disguise since it compelled the company to diversify at a time when powder was passing out of general use. As the company investigated these new possibilities vigorously, their loss of sales revenue from civilian explosives showed them the perils of relying on a single kind of product in a regulated market.

With their usual secrecy, the company began to move toward diversification. On the outbreak of World War I in 1914, Dupont switched to large-scale munitions making, with shifts working around the clock. Although the United States did not enter the war until April 1916, Dupont supplied military explosives to the Allies from the outset, providing 40 percent of the smokeless powder used by the Allies in the conflict. Dupont enlarged their plants and work force to cope with demand while continuing to move into new fields outside explosives such as paints and dyes, and greatly expanding its organic chemicals department. At the war's end, Dupont terminated all of its military explosives activities, except for two plants retained in the interests of national security. The armistice of 1918 was a signal for accelerated expansion into new peacetime lines. By 1921, the company had five diversified industrial divisions – explosives, dyestuffs, paints and chemicals, fabrikoids (fabrics with a chemical coating), and film. By 1931, seemingly without breaking step, Dupont had moved away from explosives to become the largest chemical company in America, and the fifteenth-largest company in the country overall, a transition for which there is no parallel in modern business history.

Ultimately there would be ten diversified divisions within Dupont, each with its own general manager and sales, research and support departments, all under the general direction of a President, an Executive Committee and a Board of Directors. The members of the Executive Committee were not burdened by day-to-day administrative duties or tied to any division. They spent their time thinking of the business of the company as a corporate unit. As the Harvard Business School noted, Dupont was unique in having a group of top executives 'with time to think'.[8] Equally unusually, while most other company's boards of directors were comprised of outside nominees with little knowledge of the firm, the Dupont board was composed entirely of retired Dupont company officials who 'function as elder statesmen'.[9] The relationship between the divisions was paralleled by those between their products, which were seen as 'logically related', while all the operations within a department were described as being 'in a chemical relationship to each other'[10] and all divisions were considered related in some way, so discoveries made in one division could be easily developed in another. Dupont looked corporate, but the structure and thinking remained fundamentally familial. Indeed, from an anthropological perspective, this is not so much a business structure as a corporatized form of a segmentary lineage system – kin groups composed of related families which on one level are autonomous, and on another may cooperate for shared economic or other activities, and which 'may well consider itself one people, often enough "The People"' (Sahlins 1961: 325). One of the salient characteristics of a segmentary lineage system is the way it can operate as an organization of predatory expansion due to the cooperation it can muster, which equally describes the Dupont family on the Brandywine and the new reorganized Dupont corporation. At Dupont, the early autonomous divisions worked together with a cohesion unrivalled in American business, although common enough in anthropological accounts of tribal society.

As Dupont's existing sales and production expertise was limited to explosives, the company embarked on an interim policy of obtaining wider commercial experience and knowledge of the market by buying firms already working in its desired areas of expansion. In addition to experience, it was looking to acquire products and processes they could improve until they were able to generate products of their own. Central to the company's plans were its research laboratories. In 1904, Dupont had established two laboratories at considerable expense – the Eastern Laboratory, specializing in applied research with immediate goals such as improvement of existing chemical operations and the Experimental Laboratory which specialized in innovative or fundamental research that might open up new commercial possibilities – particularly high-risk, high-return long-term investigations not tied to existing business, with potential rewards that might justify high development costs. At this time, this degree of commitment to research – particularly fundamental research – was unparalleled in American business. Also unique was the company's support for what might be seen as a dysfunctional arrangement that contradicted conventional business models. There was considerable conflict between the two laboratories and their competing types of research objectives, briefs and budgets, but the company long resisted amalgamating the two, and when change did come, the conflict was continued –

and actually encouraged – in the form of ongoing and often heated dialogue between the Research and Development sections (Hounshell and Smith 1988b). A synergy between the two was deemed necessary for the optimal balance between idealism and pragmatism. These features of Dupont's internal organization emerged publicly at the time of the transition but, as has been seen, they had been part of private DuPont family history and culture since before the founding of the firm.

It is useful here to return to the following questions: what drove the family, and what produced the corporation? The secrecy and dangers of powder-making; the social and geographical isolation of the family; its consolidation through cousin and other forms of preferential marriage; the involvement of the family in the business – all were productive of a singular cohesiveness. Shared values and joint participation in procedures and practices became so deeply embedded in daily life that they became a form of secular ritual (see Moore and Meyerhoff 1977). Unity was enhanced by the strong identification with the past in which time was dissolved and individuals depersonalized, two further features of ritual (Bloch 1977: 287), and was also seen in the repetition of family names, and in the visual commemoration of and popular belief in the persistence of the 'family face' – the distinctive features of which look out from Dupont family portraits spanning over 200 years.[11]

To a greater or lesser degree, many of these elements are to be found in other dynasties, but the unusual aspect of Dupont is the way these values and practices were put to pragmatic use. From the very beginning, chemistry and original research – as practiced by Irénée and many of his descendants who trained as chemists – were the keystone of the Dupont powder business. This research was seen by the family as an ongoing process, with continual refinements being made to give Dupont powder an edge over competing products. For a family and company so closely identified with a single product, its virtual loss was potentially destructive, yet the transition was accomplished with spectacular success. Business history has been unable to provide an explanation for this, but anthropology can. By reifying research, the company was able to preserve a family-rooted sense of mission and a unity of purpose in the face of an uncertain future. Instead of powder, research now became the core practice and value. By de-centering the actual product upon which the enterprise had been founded, and transferring the symbolic and historic connotations from the object to the process of research, the company and family were able to accommodate both continuity and change.

At Dupont, both the kinship structure and what Yanagisako calls the sentiments and culture of kinship were transferred into an internal corporate culture in which cohesiveness and cooperation were emphasized and the metaphor of family was constantly evoked, being applied even to products, as in 'the Dupont family of fibres'. The fact that the family succession crisis came in the fourth generation and not the third as is usually the case is not, I think, accidental. As with the Rothchilds (Kuper 2001) and with the Mitsuis, the pre-eminent business dynasty of pre-war Japan (Roberts 1983), cousin marriages and other practices counteracted the centrifugal tendencies so that the family remained intact for an additional generation, long enough for the culture of kinship and family to become more firmly embedded in the business. It is easy to see how this kinship-based system then 'emerged' and was corporatized at Dupont, and how easily it would have taken root, seeming perfectly 'natural' and 'the way things are done around here'. Indeed, without reference to the underlying kinship structure, it is difficult to imagine how Dupont's corporate organization and move to diversification could have been devised or implemented. The business historian Alfred D. Chandler Jr. (1972, 1978) suggests that the Dupont divisions came into being to accommodate diversification, but this begs the question of why the form was not adopted at other firms which diversified. The Dupont family member who was key to the diversification was Pierre S. Dupont, who Chandler casts as a paradigm of scientific management, but who was in fact the family 'kin-keeper' (Firth *et al.* 1969), collector of Dupont family history materials, whose archive forms the core of the family and early company records at Hagley. As Hounshell (1990) makes clear, Dupont family history and precedent rather than 'modernity' was the basis for the practices that Pierre S. Dupont introduced to the re-configured company. Over a long time, the family's continued presence in the top echelons of the corporation helped to ensure a continuity and commitment to the family ethos (Rumm 1989: xi). In the heyday of 'scientific management', family firms were considered old-fashioned, an early and primitive stage in the evolution of the modern corporation. However, the latter part of the twentieth century saw a rise in the number of family firms, especially in the face of globalization, which family firms and their networks cope with extremely well, and they are recognized as sources of innovation, and of stability in difficult economic times. If the problems of family succession can be managed successfully, even when the family no longer works in the firm but exercises control through share ownership, studies show that family firms do better than non-family concerns (Anderson and Reeb 2003) because of their internal dynamics and strong culture.

Specific historical events also influenced Dupont. The anti-trust suit effectively spelled the end of Dupont's formal involvement with vertical integration, but not its *informal* involvement, which can only be understood in the following way. A proprietary – wholly owned and trademarked – product protected by patents is, as Noble (1977) notes, essentially a monopoly by legal means. By developing their own products through original research, creating a market for them, and dominating the market through the continuing promotion of a product that undergoes continual refinement and development, stimulating competition instead of suppressing it, the company was and is able to pursue its traditional objectives without breaching government regulations.

Personal factors and events that emerge in the Dupont narratives no doubt influenced and motivated early family members, but a larger dynamic drove the family and corporate vision. As revealed in the alternative narrative of before the firm began, to the early Duponts, science – however revered – was the means to an end. That end was not the simple profit-maximizing motive attributed to capitalists, although it would be naive to claim that this was entirely absent. However, and uniquely, in the early communal enterprise, the paternalistic community of workers, the later paternalistic corporation, its commitment to free enterprise and its public identification with the nation, national goals and transcendent virtues, can be seen the principles of the physiocrats. As Pierre Samuel the patriarch put it in 1792, speaking of agriculture which he had assumed would be the focus of his envisioned American colony, but equally applicable to the family's eventual powder-making business and later the family company:

> I found the earth and the waters are the unique source of all riches ... These bases ... appeared to be so important for the human Race that all the obligation to disseminate the knowledge of them and to apply them as much as I could to the government of nations and particularly to the well-being of my Country seemed to me a veritable mission, for which I was accountable to God, to humanity and to my fellow citizens.... I thought less of Fortune and Glory – the hope for which had first determined me to work – than of the felicity, the prosperity to which I could raise my country ... such is the sentiment that since that time has directed my entire life.
>
> (Dupont 1984: 213–214)

Critics may see in this an apologia for capitalism if one were needed, but whether or not this is the case, I believe it also explains the company's distinctive grandeur of vision and sense of purpose, and its tradition of social responsibility, almost of paternalistic *noblesse oblige*, that was so much a part of the early Brandywine community, and long continued to find expression in the family's charitable works, the company's civic patronage and the way the company perceived its commercial mission. What drove the Dupont family and then the company was not simple profiteering, but a profound and complex vision that embraced family values, the scientific legacy of Lavoisier and the obligation to continue the scientific mission of Irénée. Even more fundamentally, following physiocratic principles, the company was built on the belief that monopoly and big business – as the natural outcome of successful enterprise – were not bad things in themselves so long as they were able to provide products 'at the lowest prices consistent with uniformly high quality', thereby improving the general good. E.I. du Pont de Nemours and Company was, and Hagley still is, Pontiana.

3

DUPONT'S FAMILY OF FIBERS AND THE BIRTH OF LYCRA

Textile Fibers became one of the most successful of Dupont's diversified divisions (Hounshell and Smith 1988b), dominating the field of synthetic fibers in America and abroad. Of all the company's new divisions, Textile Fibers was arguably closest to the ancestral Dupont model – a cohesive, creative, committed, proactive organization that depended on scientific research and was imbued with the principles and ideology of family. Ultimately there were seven members of what Dupont called it's 'family of fibers' – rayon, acetate, nylon, Dacron (polyester), Orlon (acrylic), Neoprene and Lycra. As Charles O. Holliday, then CEO of Dupont, said of synthetic fibers in 2002: 'We're not just the leader in this industry. We, more than anybody, created this industry.'[1]

Before Synthetic Fibers

In 1900, everyday life in the industrialized world was largely reliant on the age-old natural trinity of animal–vegetable–mineral. Natural fibers and materials such as wool, cotton, silk, linen, hemp/jute and other plants, bristles, fur, skins, bones and other animal products, wood, stone and minerals were used in everything from cloth and household goods to the necessities of industry and commerce. Beginning in the eighteenth century, the processes and technology of the Industrial Revolution had transformed many aspects of production, notably spinning and weaving, which in turn altered everyday life. Cloth has always been used to display hierarchy and status, and in the days of hand-weaving and artisanal production, fine fabrics were the preserve of the elite. Now able to be manufactured quickly and cheaply, printed and patterned textiles for clothing and the home became accessible to an ever-increasing number of consumers among the rapidly growing middle-classes that emerged during the sweeping social changes of the nineteenth century. As a result, new ways of dressing and a greater elaboration of dress generally came into being which required high levels of care and maintenance. These were supplied by the large numbers of people who were employed as domestic servants in middle-class and elite homes, where they carried out a demanding regime of soaking, washing, airing, drying, bleaching, dying, ironing, starching, altering, stretching and reshaping garments made of natural fibers.

By the beginning of the twentieth century, textile limitations and new possibilities were becoming apparent. Limitations included supply, with natural products subject to periodic fluctuations caused by factors such as environmental pressures and war. Population growth promised future shortages. Natural-fiber processing appeared to have reached its optimal level. No further technological improvements seemed possible and natural fibers and materials were proving inadequate to the new performance-related requirements of accelerating development. Buoyed up by the rising tide of scientific research and discovery, producers began to wonder – instead of coping with the limitations of the old natural materials, why not invent entirely new ones? New materials invented and developed in laboratories.

This was an enterprise for which, as we saw in Chapter 2, Dupont were ideally placed. After the loss of the anti-trust suit in 1911, Dupont became interested in products that could be processed in their existing powder plants using machinery now lying idle, using their touchstone nitrocellulose technology. After their long involvement with it, Dupont felt a sense of ownership of nitrocellulose which, typically, it asserted in terms of family and heritage, as seen in this passage from Dupont's *History of the Textile Fibers Department*, which links the firm's founder directly to man-made fibers, and draws the new enterprise firmly into the family network:

> Wood and water were essential elements for Eleuthère Irénée du Pont when in 1802 he launched the enterprise that now bears his name.... When cellulose – from wood and cotton – began its career as a chemical raw material in 1845 as 'guncotton', du Pont ... had a natural and keen interest in its development. Thus it is no surprise that the du Pont company began modest investigations of existing processes for making artificial silk as early as 1909.[2]

Synthetic Fibers and the Dupont Fiber Chain

The textile archives clarify Dupont's unique methods – so confusing on the ethnographic level – that arose directly from monopoly lawsuits. To avoid the problem in future, Dupont's extraordinary production and sales policies now involved actively promoting the Dupont name to consumers and doing extensive market research while almost never actually selling anything direct to end-use consumers.[3] As an explosives maker, Du Pont had been vertically integrated, beginning with the raw materials, then manufacturing both the semi-finished and final product, distributing and selling it to customers, albeit often in bulk. With their new diversified divisions, Dupont devised an approach that involved cutting out all but the first two stages in the chain, while still remaining involved in the total trajectory. Dupont would take basic raw materials and transform them into technologically advanced materials or processes. These they would sell on to their direct customers – independent manufacturers or fabricators – who would make them up into final end-use products to be sold on through wholesalers and retailers – Dupont's customers' customers – to the consumer. The number of links in the chain depended on the product. In a vertically integrated commodity chain, the product is moved along a chain by the traditional mechanics of production, distribution and sale. Dupont's chain was far more complex. Although it now only sold its product directly to the first link in the chain – its customers – Dupont provided the impetus for the chain as a whole, expediting the movement of the product that contained its product along the chain in a number of ways. The fiber chain linked Dupont, who invented and developed the fibers, to spinners, weavers or knitters, dyers, finishers, cutters, makers, retail stores and the staff who sold products containing Dupont fibers to the consumer. It is helpful to visualize the process as a fiber, itself in a state of change, moving along a trajectory from invention to consumption, pushed by Dupont from behind and pulled by Dupont from the front.

Ultimately, the foundation of Dupont's fiber chain was uniqueness. Almost from the beginning they invented and developed all their fibers themselves, and kept improving them, so they always had something new to offer. Although they later licensed the making of some of their fibers to other producers, initially Dupont were the sole makers of their fibers, a de facto monopoly which they enhanced in other ways. Where it had once sought to eliminate competition, the company now aimed to stimulate it by offering their customers innovative products and unrivalled technical and publicity support that would enable them to gain an edge over their rivals – and allow Dupont to keep ahead of their own rivals, other synthetic fiber producers such as Courtaulds (Handley 1999). Clients were tied to Dupont not by restrictive contracts, but by voluntary self-interest arising from the benefits that association with Dupont would bring. This unusual – even anomalous – system has passed without remark in the business history literature, and has never been fully described. It does not appear in official histories of Dupont, customers and competitors rarely have knowledge of its workings as a whole, and members of the public are generally unaware of it. It contradicts most of the conventional principles of modern corporate organization; indeed, it would be impossible to generate so distinctive a system from purely logical premises. But it worked brilliantly.

'A Woman's World'

At the beginning of its involvement with synthetic fibers, the company's public image underwent a dramatic shift in orientation and identity. During the explosives period, Dupont's customers had been male, and its orientation and identity masculine. However, public sentiment against big business had re-emerged after World War I and, while all major corporations were targeted, Dupont drew particular criticism because, as makers of munitions, they were associated in the public mind with the death and destruction of the recent conflict and implicitly blamed for them, especially after the extent of Dupont's

Figure 3.1 'The Chemical Engineer', courtesy of Hagley Museum and Library.

wartime profits became known. Concerned that negative public opinion might impact adversely on the success of the company's new diversified products, Dupont launched its first corporate advertising campaign. The series of advertisements that Dupont released in 1922 to counter the anti-war backlash introduced an iconic figure – the Chemical Engineer – holding a test tube to the light, the bringer of betterment for all through science. The Chemical Engineer also symbolized the Dupont family and company, their shared chemical heritage and commitment to ongoing research. In a radical departure in Dupont policy, the advertising campaign was intended to appeal to women.

By the 1920s, women had gained the vote, taken up driving cars, and were increasingly entering the business world, even ousting male stenographers. Movies and radio fed the demand for stylish clothes and goods for the home. Not only were women beginning to earn their own money, they increasingly took on the role of purchasing agents for the whole family. The company set out to capture this emerging market:

> now that women had the asking power, there was almost no end to the good things women demanded of industry and especially its chemical branch. Having served with distinction the nation's pioneers, protectors and builders, Du Pont and chemistry now prepared to face up to this new and exacting challenge of the Twenties.
>
> (Du Pont Company 1952: 91)

Even before they were fully established in the field, Dupont worked hard to associate itself in the public mind with women. This was more than a commercial opportunity. Becoming associated with the feminine/private/domestic sphere was a means of symbolic transformation by which the negative associations of munitions, explosives, big business and the masculine/public arena for which the company had previously been known could be left behind. It was at this time that references to powder-making were left off the map of Hagley drawn for the endpapers of the *Autobiography*.

At the end of World War I, Dupont purchased the American rights to a French cellulose fiber and opened its first artificial silk fiber factory. When Dupont's salesmen went out on the road with the new fiber, they encountered immediate opposition from the New England textile mills who specialized in cotton and wool. Declaring that 'a synthetic fiber is a fly-by-night novelty', they castigated Dupont's salesmen for 'wasting their precious time talking about something that was artificial and therefore ridiculous'.[4] Although imported artificial silk sold well and was widely used by manufacturers for underwear and hosiery, Dupont discovered that 'art silk' was seen by the public as a cheap and often shoddy substitute for natural silk – not attractive to a company whose powder had been synonymous with quality and who sought to transfer this cachet to its new diversified products. Changing the name of the fiber from 'artificial silk' to 'rayon' did not improve matters. In addition, the fiber produced using the French formula was proving extremely difficult for textile spinners and weavers and clothing manufacturers to work with.

Instead of continuing in the face of trade and consumer opposition, Dupont decided to reverse the process. The company already had unrivaled expertise with cellulose as a chemical raw material, as well as an ongoing program of cellulose research and advanced engineering technology, to which they now added the new field of market research. Instead of attempting to fix a flawed product or launching new ones without knowing if they were likely to succeed, Dupont would now find out what women wanted, and then use chemistry to develop fibers that would deliver the desired qualities and capabilities. Being synthetic, cellulose was 'capable of continuing change and improvement [in the laboratory], a fact that was at once its forte and promise' (Dutton 1942: 308), giving it a huge potential advantage over natural fibers. It was this aspect of synthetic fibers – the fact that they could be invented 'to order' – that gave rise to the company's intensive and unique use of market research over the years, which can be seen as a natural extension of their information-gathering activities during the powder era. Dupont's first effort involved funding a national poll of 10,000 women to find out what women wanted from artificial silk. This, the survey revealed, was not another kind of silk, but completely new kinds of outerwear materials that were resistant to soiling, easy to clean and care for, that held their shape, were durable but also soft, were comfortable in warm weather, smart in appearance and reasonably priced. But this was only the beginning.

'Resilience' in fibers, for example, was a quality that emerged again and again as something spinners, weavers, manufacturers and consumers all wanted from new textiles. This was relayed to the textile fiber research laboratories, who were expected to transmute desires into fibers, but 'resilience' was a vague term. What exactly did 'resilience' mean to consumers? Were resilient fibers meant to never change their shape, or were they supposed to spring back into their original shape after wear and cleaning? Were resilient fibers meant to be supple or firm? Should they be designed for use in woven or knitted fabrics? Resilience generated a research trail that lasted for years, cost millions of dollars, and generated internal debate over the relative merits of different chemical processes and technologies. Many fiber samples were produced, refined, rejected, produced from scratch again, tested, sampled by customers, returned for modification and re-tested until the final fibers were selected for commercial development and Orlon and Dacron were finally launched – outcomes of the fiber-creation process that the public never sees.

Expressed preferences for qualities like resilience reflected the emergent postwar lifestyle in which unprecedented leisure and mobility, along with a rising number of women going to work outside the home, led to a demand for easy living, easy shopping and easy care. Domestic service declined in the interwar years, and largely disappeared during World War II, leaving a generation of women who were unwilling or unable to undertake the work and expense involved in caring for natural fibers. Yet, despite these nascent social trends and expressed desires, Dupont found that, in practice – a classic example of conscious and unconscious models, or the difference between what people say they want and what they really want – the majority of manufacturers and consumers remained resistant to the idea of synthetic fibers and fabrics generally. The company discovered that, in order to be successful, it had to do more than invent and sell new fibers – it had to sell new ways of living, and new ways of working and thinking about cloth to the public and the trade alike. Dupont had to create culture in order to sell cloth (O'Connor 2005, 2008).

The company's extensive collection of marketing, research and promotional materials offer a rare and invaluable opportunity to see how this was done. As O'Barr (1994: 201) has noted:

> market research, unlike academic social science research, is usually proprietary. It amounts to a private sociology and psychology of the consumer society that will never be available beyond very narrow limits.... Because neither the advertising agencies nor the companies they represent are historical archives, most research reports are destroyed.

Fortunately, Dupont's Textile Fibers Department archive includes not only consumer documents, sales records and market research, but also notebooks and other material from the scientific laboratories that invented and refined the fibers, giving a rare insight into science as a coherent human activity, and into 'research trails' – the private delays, frustrations and difficulties of scientific research which are often concealed in corporate and scientific public culture (Holmes 1990).

While the properties of natural fibers like silk and cotton had been known for millennia, those of synthetic fibers were largely unknown even to their inventors, and required completely new types of industrial machinery as well. Instead of simply selling the fiber to the mills – a challenge in itself in view of their resistance – Dupont had to provide an unprecedented level of technical support. While helping the customers to solve their problems had always been a part of Dupont's business, synthetic fibers presented a host of new challenges. These included quality monitoring, the recommendation of product improvements needed to meet competition, helping customers to cope with the new textile technology, teaching customers how to use Dupont fibers, feeding back information about textile costs and adjudicating customer claims. As one salesman put it, instead of being 'just a salesman' with order book in hand, a Dupont fiber salesman had to be a merchandising specialist, technical service man, huckster and jack-of-all-trades to serve his customers' every need in the way the powder salesmen had done.

Sales and technical support to Dupont's direct customers were only part of the chain. Because synthetic fibers were entirely new, demand for them had to be created at every point in the selling chain. Dupont's direct customers were the spinners and weavers, but the selling chain itself did not stop there. Fabric manufacturers sold the fabric on to garment makers or cutters, who in turn sold their goods to retail outlets ranging from large chain stores and mail-order catalog houses to small specialty shops nationwide. All had to be persuaded to take on the new goods containing Dupont fibers and taught how to sell them effectively. And finally, the women who walked into the shops had to want – or at least know about – the new fibers and fabrics and their advantages in the first place.

Using the artificial silk survey as a template, Dupont in time built up a textile marketing department unparalleled in the trade. There were surveys of particular types of garments or household goods, surveys of fashion trends and colors, and general information on what consumers wanted. This information was passed on to the technical, research, development and sales departments to generate better products, to selected manufacturers to keep them abreast with trends, and to retailers to enable them to sell products with Dupont fibers more effectively. Surveys were backed up by advertising support. Dupont would prepare standardized advertisements for shops and stores to run in local newspapers consisting of blocks with standard illustrations and headlines, but spaces left blank for the store's name and local details, thereby saving the store the costs of an advertising or commercial art agency's fee. Dupont provided manufacturers with free garment swing tags that displayed the Dupont logo or fiber name prominently, and sew-in garment labels also carrying the Dupont name. Dupont also undertook joint advertisements and promotions with leading manufacturers and stores, and sent out press releases on new fibers and fashions using them, which received attention in the trade and consumer press, benefiting Dupont, their customers and their customers' customers. No fiber competitor could offer this service, and no customer could mount such a comprehensive service on their own. It provided a powerful incentive to work with Dupont, and considerably enhanced the 'value' of Dupont fibers which, as with the Dupont powder of old, offered high quality at high prices.

Fiber Expansion

At the end of 1939, Dupont's popularity with women increased with the invention of nylon (Handley 1999). May 14, 1940 was the day when nylon stockings – five million pairs – first went on sale. By sundown, all five million had been sold, after riots in many shops.[5] The sensational appearance of nylon on the market, as described in Hounshell and Smith's 'The Nylon Drama' (1988), available online, vindicated the company's commitment to a combination of pure science idealism and pragmatic corporatism. Nylon signaled the end of Dupont's transitional fiber strategy, and established the pattern for all the company's future work on textiles. In future, Dupont would only work with fibers they had invented and developed themselves. Nylon and the other big textile discoveries at Dupont came out of the Pioneering Research Department, based from 1950 in laboratories on a bluff overlooking Hagley. For as long as they continued to produce it, Dupont never 'finished' with a fiber. As had been the case with powder, the Dupont laboratories were constantly working on new refinements and applications of their fibers which were then patented. Patenting was central to the Dupont operation, and a department was maintained specifically to prepare them. Every Dupont invention, fiber and process was ring-fenced with patents. In the first 160 years of its existence, the company was granted 13,000 patents and these were rigorously enforced and vigorously defended against infringement.

The development of nylon took thirteen years and cost an unprecedented $27,000,000. Nylon was used in a variety of end-products, from tooth brushes to tennis rackets, across a number of Dupont's diversified divisions. This showed one of the strengths of Dupont's diversified lineage structure, in which a single new research discovery could benefit many divisions, but could also stimulate productive competition between them for the best and most profitable applications. The association of the Dupont name with scientific research and progress was reinforced by the company's slogan, coined in 1935, which became a national catchphrase: 'Better Things for Better Living, Through Chemistry.' To the company, it was more than an advertising slogan. It was, as the *Dupont Magazine* put it, 'a publicly uttered promise by Du Pont; a commitment to probe the mysteries of chemistry in search of discoveries that will expand and enrich the quality of people's lives everywhere'.[6] By now, the Dupont oval was seen everywhere, giving a visual unity to Dupont's diverse enterprises. It appeared, the company noted, on cases, drums, barrels, tankers, trucks, cans, folders, brochures, broadsides, leaflets, letterheads, envelopes, checks. It was 'seen at fairs, in moving pictures and radio studios and reproduced in every medium from printer's ink to neon'.[7] Increasingly, the Dupont oval was seen on labels attached to clothing and underwear. Dupont only made fibers, not cloth or finished garments. But because Dupont labels went into garments made of cloth that used Dupont fiber, this distinction was often lost on the buying public, who began to look for the Dupont label and logo in clothing and underwear as a mark of quality, as was the case with other diversified Dupont products that were rapidly becoming the stuff of everyday life.

Within textiles, Dupont initially concentrated on developing nylon for use in a single type of garment – hosiery. Market research had established the need for stockings that were sheer and durable enough to compete with silk,

Figure 3.2 'The Chemical Girl of 1940', cover of the *Du Pont Magazine*, June 1940, courtesy of Hagley Museum and Library.

but stable in price and more certain of supply. The association between women, chemistry and Dupont was highlighted on the cover of the June 1940 issue of the company's *Dupont Magazine,* showing a young woman smartly dressed top to toe in Dupont fibers, standing in a test tube against the background of the World Fair and captioned 'The Chemical Girl of 1940'. She was a fitting partner for the Chemical Engineer, the pair paralleling the period's gender roles: man as producer, woman as consumer.[8]

After World War II

Following America's entry into World War II in December 1941 after the attack on Pearl Harbor, most of Dupont's textile fiber production was diverted to the war effort, but fundamental research continued, ensuring that the company would have new products and refinements of existing products to commercialize when the war was over. As it had after World War I, Dupont emerged from the conflict economically buoyant and substantially larger, with employment up 21 percent on prewar levels. Anticipating a surge of popular anti-war feeling and resentment of wartime profits, Dupont launched a public culture initiative as it had after World War I, commissioning art with patriotic themes from Brandywine School artists for Dupont's annual calendar which was sent to all of Dupont's trade customers and distributed to the public through trade outlets. There was a different painting for every month, each reinforcing the links between the company and the nation's heritage.[9] Among the twelve subjects portrayed in the 1942 Dupont calendar were General George Washington at Fort Necessity during the French and Indian Wars of 1754, the inauguration of Washington as first President of the United States in 1789, and the Treaty between Indians and the Pilgrims at Plymouth, Massachusetts in 1621.

On the business front, the company's postwar objective was to maintain high levels of employment and production by bringing out a constant flow of new products. Dupont introduced its Orlon acrylic fiber in 1948, its Dacron polyester fiber in 1951 and its wash-and-wear finish for fabrics in 1952. Behind the scenes in the Textile Fibers Department and its laboratories, there was an on-going debate on whether they should push to discover one big product – the 'new nylon' – or concentrate on developing new applications of fundamental research already carried out. Meanwhile, in the Textile Sales Department, intensive efforts were underway to find more applications and markets for fibers for which an initial use had already been established. With rayon and acetate, Dupont had first developed the fiber for use in lingerie, underwear and hosiery, later extending it into outwear. Further work on nylon had continued through the war in the expectation that, after the war was over, Dupont would find new garment uses for nylon, which had originally been used only for hosiery, girdles and brassieres.

Figure 3.3 Nylon Gives You Something Extra, courtesy of Hagley Museum and Library.

As they had in an earlier postwar period, Dupont intensified their identification with women, disassociating themselves with war and munitions. As John Gunther, the influential journalist and popular historian, wrote in *Inside America* (1947: 635):

What really makes Du Pont, the company, live and breathe is – women! Its history is a development from dynamite to nylon, at least in times of peace. Of course, explosives are still an important part of the business, but its biggest department is Rayon, which includes nylon and cellophane.... So by a strange paradox, the women, not the men of the world, are the ultimate determinant of Du Pont policy. Much more than dynamite, the company rests on housewives.

As with powder in the old days, Dupont aimed to sell its textile fibers and other diversified products in bulk, for consumption by the largest possible number of customers, direct or indirect. For this reason, essential mass-market clothes that everyone wore, and in which factors like ease of care and laundering were paramount – garments such as men's shirts, hosiery and women's underwear – were the ideal uses for their fibers. Over the years, Dupont commissioned many market reports on women's slips, women's panties and men's underwear and socks, and the company then began to look at outerwear. Style was becoming important in the growing consumer market, and Dupont felt they had to expand into the outerwear market to sustain postwar sales of their fibers.

In order to assess the potential of this new field, in 1952 Dupont's Textile Fibers Department commissioned one of the most detailed surveys ever undertaken by the company. Entitled *The Dress Industry*, its brief was to determine the nature and dimensions of the largest single segment of the apparel trade, which consumed $200 billion worth of fibers annually.[10] The women's wardrobes revealed in *The Dress Industry* bear little resemblance to the contents of contemporary closets, and give insights into a now-vanished way of life. Women of the early 1950s mostly wore dresses, skirts less often, and trousers almost never. There were several kinds of dresses no longer seen, such as 'house dresses' or 'wash dresses' – not housecoats or old dresses – but new dresses which were made to be only worn indoors. There was no equivalent of today's man-tailored business suit – women's suits were soft, feminine, colorful and often accessorized with matching hats. There was no active sportswear. Coats were elaborate and women owned several. Regardless of season, occasion or age of the wearer, the standard look for women was formal, well-groomed, 'grown-up' and controlled. In terms of turnover, *The Dress Survey* identified the 'better' or popular-price mid-market dress, accounting for 55 percent of the total dress market, as the ideal sector for Dupont to target, but time and time again the report emphasized the difficulties of producing fibers for the fashion market, warning that, while easy-care and wrinkle-resistant properties were useful, neither designers nor consumers would sacrifice style for utility to achieve a fashionable look. The report concluded that, because of fashion's whims, the dress industry was unattractive from a yarn producer's standpoint, and its only positive suggestion was that prospects might be improved if Dupont could get Paris designers to help in developing and using new synthetic fabrics. Undeterred, Dupont decided to pursue the fashion market. From now on, the company's efforts were split between linking synthetics with style by developing links with French fashion houses and the nascent American fashion industry centered in New York (Blaszczyk 2006) on the one hand, and three other main objectives on the other. These were: promoting the functionality of their new fibers to the general public; servicing the emerging youth sector of the consumer market; and searching for the holy grail of underwear – the perfect girdle.

Will It Be Pretty? Promoting Fibers and Function

The immediate post-World War II period saw Dupont mounting a new synthetic fiber promotion initiative. Although Orlon, Dacron, nylon and wash-and-wear had all been developed in response to the wants and needs revealed through market research, when they were first introduced to the market, Dupont once again encountered trade and customer resistance. As with rayon in the 1920s, the company had to mount a new campaign to sell a new way of living and completely new kind of fibers and fabrics made from them all along the fiber chain. The new Dupont fibers would eventually transform the way clothes were worn and cared for. In the company's words:

> Back in the 1950s and 1960s, the sale of synthetic fibers had to be built in part on describing the advantages of these new fibers not only to the industry but also to the consumer. Consider such common apparel as sweaters that can be washed without shrinkage, undergarments needing no ironing, skirts and trousers with permanent pleats and creases, and outerwear staying fresh-looking despite high humidity. None of these had any meaning before the advent of nylon, Dacron and Orlon.[11]

A besetting problem for Dupont was how to convey the advantages and capabilities of these new products of scientific research in language the general public could understand and relate to. Central to Dupont's marketing research operations were special reports commissioned from a wide range of consultants to aid the company in their sales and promotion efforts. One such report was *Ideas from a Woman's Viewpoint*, commissioned from the actress and model Anita Colby for the Dupont Advertising Clinic in 1955, in which she effectively lampooned the over-use of scientific terminology in advertising consumer goods, a lesson that continues to elude many marketers of science and technology:

Why just this morning, I saw to it that I put on my 'long-chain synthetic polymeric amides', safely crossed a floor coated with a wax containing colloidal silica, took a deep breath of air deliciously cooled by dichlorofifluomethane because I was so nervous about coming here to meet you (especially those of you in the Dichlorodiphenylthrichloroethene Division) – and have found that all of you, dressed so handsomely in your acrylic fibers, formed by a polymer of acrylonitrile – have put me completely at ease. Whew! I only wish your language did too.... For instance – just come to a woman all excited and say, 'I've just invented a cyclotronovariegatomon!' and not a bit fazed, she'll just look at you innocently with her baby blues and ask, 'Darling, will it be pretty?'[12]

The public found it easier to relate to performances staged by a stalwart of Dupont's fiber promotion initiative, Charles H. Rutledge, Manager of Information Services for the Textile Fibers Department. Rutledge's hobby was collecting old-time household equipment, especially antique flatirons which, he said, symbolized the tedious task that had traditionally been women's most disliked household chore. Rutledge used his flatirons as props for the lectures he gave to women's groups across the country on the theme of 'Your Mothers and Grandmothers Never Had It So Good', which dwelt on the many Dupont products that had made life easier and more enjoyable for women, emphasizing Dupont's pioneering development of synthetic fibers that freed women from the drudgery of ironing. 'There has been a complete transition from the once inflexible routine of wash-on-Monday, iron-on-Tuesday-and-maybe-work-furiously-Wednesday-to-finish-the-job', Rutledge would say, going on to extol the virtues of Dupont's easy-care fabrics that could be put through an automatic washer and emerge in less than an hour, ready to wear. At an appropriate point in his presentation, Rutledge would step behind a screen, change into a robe, and then toss his wash-and-wear suit into the washing machine that was one of his props, continuing to talk while the suit was being laundered. Later Rutledge would change back into his freshly washed suit and finish his talk.[13] Audiences were fascinated, and the talk was filmed and shown nationally to retailers and consumers.

With textile innovations at their height, Dupont mounted a national campaign in the new medium of television, specifically intended to raise the profile of synthetic fibers, to boost women's confidence about using them, and to promote the ideas of science and progress generally. The first Dupont television program, *Cavalcade of America*, began as a successful radio series of the same name, which pioneered the use of drama as a promotional advertising device. This excerpt from Shooting Script #68, 'Modern Clothes for Modern Living', broadcast in 1954 is representative:[14]

Main title. Opening music behind. Dissolve to:

Full shot of a 1900 bedroom. Luggage is piled up in a corner of the room and men's and women's clothes of the period are scattered over all the furniture, the bed, etc. A man is struggling to get one steamer trunk closed. His wife hovers nearby, ready to hand him a trunk strap.

WOMAN: Uh ... try sitting on it, dear ...

The man nods impatiently and does so, but the trunk still doesn't close.

WOMAN: Be careful! I don't want to spend the whole two weeks' vacation ironing clothes!
MAN: Well, do you have to take along everything you own?
WOMAN: What do you mean everything I own? There are four suits of yours and a dozen shirts in that trunk!

Cut to medium close-up of presenter in studio set.

PRESENTER: That happy little scene was probably repeated many years ago when bulky, uncomfortable, hard-to-care-for clothes were the order of the day. Now, suppose we move this same couple forward to the present day ...

Dissolve to full shot of a modern-style bedroom. The man and woman are now dressed in good-looking, comfortable traveling clothes. Two light suitcases are open and they are packing.

MAN: Let's see ... two suits ... my sports jacket and slacks ... a couple of shirts ... oh yes, and a sports shirt. Ready, honey?

Cut to: shot of man and woman. She is packing underthings in her suitcase.

WOMAN: In a minute ...

She closes suitcase.

MAN: Hey, won't those things get all messed up?
WOMAN: If they do, most of the wrinkles will hang right out. Come on!

Dissolve to medium shot of presenter in set.

PRESENTER: Yes, they need to take only one suitcase apiece – yet they're going to be both comfortable and well-dressed, the whole two weeks they're away. How do they do it? Well it isn't just a change of styles since 1900. In fact, fabrics have changed just as much as styles – and the development of versatile man-made fibers, such as those made by Du Pont, has helped make many advances possible … And the skill of America's clothing manufacturers, combined with Du Pont research, will *continue* to bring you advances in clothing practicality, good looks and comfort … another contribution by Du Pont to …

Cut to shot of the Du Pont oval (logo) and Du Pont slogan, repeated voice over.

'Better Things for Better Living … Through Chemistry'

Later in the 1950s, the *Cavalcade of America* evolved into a general drama program called the *Du Pont Show of the Month*, which consisted of a short information feature on Dupont's research and new inventions along with a dramatic play aimed at women from middle-income households with an annual income of $4,000–$7,000, and with an educational level of high school or better, from either white- or blue-collar households, who were regarded by the company as the main potential consumer group for hosiery, foundation garments, underwear and outerwear made of the new fibers.[15] The star was June Allyson, an aspirational figure for this group, a girl-next-door stage and screen actress described by Ginger Rogers as 'the girl every man wants to marry and the girl every woman wants as a friend'. The shows were broadcast weekly on CBS-TV on Monday night, between the traditional washing day and ironing day, when women would be most receptive. The storylines were chosen for their 'special feminine appeal' – one of the first episodes concerned a woman's struggle to avenge her husband's death – but the main feature of the shows from the company's point of view was Miss Allyson's size-5 wardrobe, everything in it specially designed 'by the well-known Hollywood couturier Howard Shoup', using fabrics containing Dupont fibers.

To supplement its marketing and scientific research, Dupont commissioned social research by leading social analysts of the day, to keep Dupont personnel well-informed of new social trends, essential during the years after World War II when rising income and population levels, new roles for women, and increasing opportunities for leisure and recreation began to transform the consumer market. At a 1955 Dupont advertising clinic, James A. Linen, publisher of *Time* magazine, spoke of what he called the 'revolution in education', which would see an increase of 60 percent in high school enrollments in the 1960s, and a huge rise in college enrollments. Linen warned: 'We simply dare not under-estimate the impact this will have on tomorrow's consumers, on their tastes and values, and on their own absorption with and of new ideas.'[16] These consumers of tomorrow were the young Boomers. Another such event was 'Your Customer in a World of Change',[17] a 1958 forum, with talks by the anthropologist Clyde Kluckhohn of Harvard

University on *Changing Values*, by sociologists Samuel Stouffer of Harvard University on *Changes in Living Patterns* and William F. Whyte of Cornell University on *Problems of Intercultural Communication*, and Edward Gudeman of Sears Roebuck and Company on *The Retail Merchant in a Changing United States*. Among the changing values highlighted by Kluckhohn were the rise of diversity, which he saw as becoming one of the organizing principles in the culture of the United States, arising from the 'bewildering rapidity of change', and a shift in 'the ideal for American women and her place in society'. As a result of the withering of the Puritan ethic, Kluckhohn said, men were seldom patriarchs any more. Although women in the United States were competing in the occupational system, and middle-class men were beginning to take on domestic duties such as cooking, there was a dissatisfaction among women that some found puzzling. Women were no longer content to be just the 'housewives' of whom Gunther had written ten years previously. As Kluckhohn noted: 'Some foreign observers comment, especially foreign women, that American women seem to them to have absolutely everything and yet they don't seem to be entirely contented.'[18] Within a few years, with the rise of the Women's Liberation movement, American women would attempt to truly 'have it all'. But, in 1958, it was difficult to foresee how this would impact on the consumer market and on production.

Dupont also commissioned studies in the new field of motivational research, which applied psychoanalytic techniques and concepts to the study of consumer behavior. Motivational research was widely used by American corporations in the 1950s and 1960s, decried by critics (Packard 1957) as manipulative techniques of dubious morality, and hailed by supporters as a scientific means of understanding the new mass consumer market. Representative motivational research studies include 'The Psychology of Breakfast Cereals', 'A Study of the Psychological and Sociological Functions of Gasoline Stations' and 'The Difficulty of Selling Christmas Cards in August – A Psychological Analysis'. All of these were carried out for various corporate clients by Ernest Dichter (1907–1991), the 'Father of Motivational Research', a Vienna-trained psychologist who came to America in 1938, and whose papers are in the archive at Hagley. Among them are studies Dichter undertook for Dupont, including 'A Motivational Research Study of Sales and Advertising Problems of Nylon Bed Sheets'. Dupont also commissioned studies from less eminent figures, and from its own in-house marketing department, one being the study entitled *Research Basis for the Self Confidence Theme* (1959)[19] which gives insight into the rigid dress codes and norms of the time. It reports that clothing 'assumes its greatest importance to consumers in terms of the social and psychological values they fulfill', the strongest and most important of which is 'self-confidence', based on 'appropriateness – as for age or occasion', on 'conformity to role or status in life –

not dressing above or below one's social level' and on 'achieving the right lines for one's figure'.

A New Consumer Market – the Young Boomer Cohort

As the company, the Textile Fibers Division and its activities grew, so did a new consumer market – the 'Baby Boom' babies, or 'Boomers'. Immediately after the war, Dupont had switched its plastics production from military equipment to baby consumables and the new high-performance fibers found a booming new market in clothes that demanded practicality rather than style – diapers, layettes, baby clothes and blankets. The progress of the young Boomers can be traced through Dupont press releases in nearly all departments. For Dupont, this was a cohort seen through stuff. There were press releases on Orlon lay-ettes for infants and quilts for toddlers; advertisements for hygienic plastic nursing bottles and unbreakable plates and cups for children; market research on potential sales of misses' panties and girls' slips in nylon tricot. Dupont plastics and other products were used in the toys that Boomers remember so fondly today. Above all, the new cohort was a prime market for Dupont's ever-increasing range of fibers, made up into fabrics and clothes that were designed to save their mothers time and effort. The mother-appeal of Dupont fibers was epitomized in *Never Too Young*, an advertisement for a frilly girl's party frock, an object of desire that was normally a nightmare to clean and press, made of easy-care fabric.

The year of 1959 would prove to be the peak birth-rate year for the Boomers, whom Dupont clearly considered their future market. As a Dupont press release of that year put it:

> Grandmothers, babysitters, brace yourself for a busy year ahead! For 1959 promises to yield a bumper crop of babies, even topping the 4,250,000 total for 1958. Statistically speaking, last year 11,643 infants arrived every 24-hour day, or 485 babies came into the world each hour. Even more specifically, every 7½ seconds someone became a proud parent. But as carriage trade increases, clothing problems decrease for this enormous group of miniature fashion plates, because of the continuing growth of infants' wear made of easy care man-made fibers such as Orlon Acrylic fiber. A boon to generous grandmothers and gift-giving godmothers – knitted creepers, lacy shawls, sturdy romper sets and many, many more items of Orlon make tempting presents for christening days and other holidays in baby's first year.[20]

Dupont saw the Boomer cohort through stuff and numbers, and it was the par-ents who made the purchasing decisions. Looking to the future, Dupont, the

Never too young to step out in easy-care Du Pont Nylon

It's 100% Du Pont nylon organdy—in party dresses that need none of yesterday's pampering. For today, thanks to nylon, even delicate-looking clothes have a practicality they've never had before. These delightful dresses can be hand-washed, need only a quick, light pressing. The detail, too—tumbles of roses, wisps of embroidery—is actually *easy* to touch up. And because of nylon's remarkable shape retention, these dresses stay crisp, fresh . . . won't wilt. When you go holiday shopping, keep in mind that, today, young beauty can be carefree, too, with nylon . . . one of Du Pont's modern-living fibers.

BETTER THINGS FOR BETTER LIVING
. . . THROUGH CHEMISTRY

Exciting new things are happening in Du Pont NYLON

Figure 3.4 *Never Too Young To Step Out in Easy-Care DuPont Nylon,* courtesy of Hagley Museum and Library.

textile trade and industry generally did not think that the demands of the emerging Boomer market when it reached adulthood would be any different to those of their parents, except with regard to population size. It was the sheer mass of the Boomer cohort and their anticipated future requirements that drove one of the Dupont Textile Division's great postwar initiatives – the search for the perfect girdle.

The Girdle

'To serve a market, fill a need' is the way a *Dupont Magazine* issue of 1980 described the long-standing objective of the company generally. This template had been set by powder explosives, the ancestral product and a commodity that was always in demand, perceived as a need rather than as a want; an indispensable product that was so taken for granted that its presence in everyday life was unquestioned. All Dupont's diversified divisions sought to come up with products that fit this template, and in the Textile Fibers Division, the ideal product – which continued to elude them – was the perfect girdle.

A girdle is a 'foundation garment', worn under clothes. In the period when Dupont was casting around for new synthetic fiber opportunities, it was taken for granted that a woman should not appear in public, and hardly in private, unless she was wearing a girdle. Although there were exceptions, and variations in private along the axes of class and wealth (see Kammen 1999), the 1940s and 1950s were generally a period of great conformity or 'normality', at least in public (Oakley 1990; Walker 2000). Cross (2000: 182) calls the 1950s the 'togetherness decade' – and girdle-wearing was something all women did together.

So completely has the girdle disappeared from general wear today that few people born after the 1970s have any experience, actual or visual, of these once ubiquitous undergarments. Heavy and clumsy, they fastened with zippers or hooks-and-eyes, or were available in 'roll-on' tubular styles. They came in unconvincing shades described as 'flesh pink' or 'peach', and were usually fitted along the front and back bottom edge with garters, to hold up stockings. There were many different kinds of girdle to go with every style of fashion, even girdles for wearing under trousers. The basic girdle went from the waist to the top of the thighs. Other models went higher, to cover the midriff, and lower, down to mid-thigh, in various combinations. There were girdles designed to be worn under pencil skirts, and girdles meant to be worn under full skirts. Many girdles incorporated brassieres so women only had to wear one foundation garment, and these types of girdle came with different styles of strap, or as strapless models. Sometimes basic girdles were worn with separate long-line bras that held in the midriff, and there were long-line girdles that went all the way from the top of the bosom to the knees.

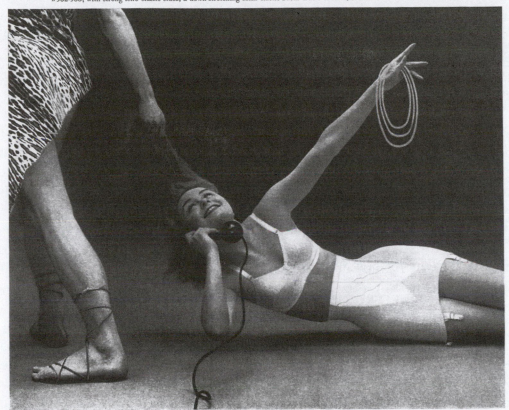

Come out of the bone age, darling…

Warner's exclusive new STA-FLAT replaces pokey bones with circular springlets

WARNER'S takes the cave-man manners out of old-fashioned girdles (poke, shove, groan), removes those long front bones that dug into your midriff. Now control's achieved with light springlets pocketed in the girdle's front panel. They're light and flexible—modern as your way of life, sensible as vitamins.

Far better control, too—STA-FLAT gives not just pinpoint support, like old-fashioned bones, but firms a greater area with lively comfort. Bend, breathe, sit ... STA-FLAT™ moves through the day with you, responds to every movement of your body ... all with unbelievable lightness. And at the same time, it gives you extra support where you need it most (midriff, waist, tummy).

You don't need to wear armor to be a charmer. Warner's is happy to give the dinosaur his due—but not on you. Come out beautifully, into the light, free whirl of today! At your nicest stores, here and in Canada.

WARNER'S®
Bras · Girdles · Corselettes

Figure 3.5 Before Lycra: advertisement for a girdle by Warner's, image courtesy of the Advertising Archives.

There is no parallel in modern textiles to the stiffness of rubberized girdle fabric, which compressed the body in a way that would now be considered intolerable, and did not correspond in any way to the strong yet supple hold, reminiscent of natural skin or muscle, that we think of today as 'stretch'. Getting into a girdle was a complex operation, described to me as 'a struggle' and 'murder' by women now in their seventies and eighties. This was the case even if the wearer was of normal weight or even thin, because to be effective the rubberized girdle had to fit very tightly, and fastening it up was awkward. If the girdle had hook-and-eye fastenings, the flesh had to be pinched, pushed and prodded out of harm's way as the edges were pulled together and fastened hook by hook. Zipper fastenings were also challenging – it was difficult to keep the edges together and pull up the zip at the same time, and in the process the flesh often got pinched painfully. Roll-on styles presented other problems. Once past the knees and lower thighs, it was very hard to pull the inflexible garments upwards. Often the effort would cause the wearer to perspire, which would make the girdle stick even more. For this reason, many women dusted themselves with talcum powder before beginning, in order to ease the girdle's progress, creating a huge demand for a product that is now largely used only for babies and by elderly ladies. The talcum also helped to absorb the perspiration that was an unavoidable part of rubberized girdle wearing. Once encased in the girdle, normal body movements like bending and sitting became awkward, eating was uncomfortable, and performing basic body functions could become problematic. One woman recalled: 'They used to say we ladies took a long time in the powder room. We weren't powdering our noses. We were struggling with our girdles.' Once a girdle was removed or lowered, it was almost impossible to get it back on, and many women remembered having to 'hold on' until they got home. Girdles were worn by women of all classes, across all income groups and regions. The only thing that varied was the quality and quantity, according to resources. All women owned several girdles, if only because they were difficult to clean and took a long time to dry, so having a selection on hand was essential.

Girdle manufacturing was one of the most profitable and dependable sectors of the garment industry. Girdle advertisements were a mainstay of women's magazines and newspapers, department stores all across the price spectrum had extensive foundation departments which were often among the most profitable in the store, there were many small shops that specialized in foundations, and girdles were huge money-spinners for mass mail order concerns like Sears Roebuck and Company. In the upmarket specialist shops, the relationship between a woman and her 'fitter' or corsetiere was compared to that between a man and his tailor. A woman built up a relationship with her fitter, who came to know her figure and its requirements intimately, having been professionally trained, often in schools run by foundation manufacturers. In the midmarket department stores, the sales personnel – always female – would be called 'salesgirls' rather than 'fitters', but they too received instructions on fitting and promotional literature from foundation-makers. Even in self-service departments, customers needed no urging to buy. No woman – young, middle-aged or old – would leave the house without wearing a girdle, and young girls were put into girdles by their mothers while they were still at school. There was no question about it. Girdles were something women *had* to own and wear.

Clothing, Culture and Control

Girdles were a significant item of mass production and mass consumption, a commodity with a firm grip on its market. But how and why did a garment that was so highly uncomfortable and restrictive come to occupy such an important position within culture and commerce?

When I asked older women who had worn girdles on a daily basis why they had done so, their replies were remarkably consistent. First, the girdle was the hallmark of respectability – a prerequisite for being considered 'dressed' or 'proper'. 'It was unthinkable not to wear one' was a frequent response. Variations of 'I don't recall anyone saying anything, it was understood that you wore a girdle. There were no "ifs" and "buts", you just did it' were common, as were statements like, 'You just did it automatically, it was the thing to do.' The second justification for wearing girdles had to do with 'health', which was often expressed in vague terms as a 'need for support', as if one would just 'flop over' without it, as one woman put it. The need to 'keep warm' was also mentioned, although girdles were worn in summer as well as in winter. The third common reason given was the need to look good in clothes, which was thought to be impossible without the aid of foundations. The most disapproved-of natural features for which the girdle was seen as the corrective were fat, sag, bulge and jiggle.

This takes us back to the culture concept, and notions of 'ideologies' and 'controlling processes' outlined in Chapter 1. As with stuff in general, the things people wear don't just happen. Because they are the intimate material interface between private and public, self and society, internal and external, clothes are especially significant forms of stuff. At all times and in all places, clothing, grooming and other bodily practices signify participation in society and acceptance of its values, or their rejection. As Sahlins (1976: 203) put it, '"Mere appearance" must be one of the most important forms of symbolic statement in western civilization.' To the people involved, what they wear and do to their bodies may seem like free choice, but choice is never free. Ultimately, it is always constrained by culture or ideologies. First, because culture and ideologies influence what is produced, and second, because they guide which of these products particular people will consume, through informal unwritten 'rules' that 'everyone knows' and takes for granted. There is no single controlling process or factor. People, ideologies, history, society, values and stuff all work upon and through each other.

For example, the market and motivational research carried out by Dupont and others in the 1950s and early 1960s uncovered much of the implicit ideology, values and 'rules' that guided consumption. In seeking to use them to sell their goods, producers were perpetuating and, to some degree, making the market, and they and their products were being perpetuated and influenced by it in return, but producers did not create the 'rules'. They were already there. And at the height of the mass-consumption and conformity of the 1950s, consumers were perpetuating the same 'rules'. In the papers in the Dupont textile archive, the phrase that occurs again and again is 'give the customer what she wants'.

In anthropological terms the girdle was, above all else, a symbol, a materialization of cultural values or ideologies, a statement in commodity form. But what exactly was it saying? There are several ways to approach this. From a political/economic perspective, one could place the girdle within the broad narratives of American business and political history, and show it to be the outcome of a confluence of factors that include phenomenal economic growth, unprecedented levels of mass production and consumption, sweeping social change and new chemical manufacturing processes. Social change is always balanced by increased social control to maintain overall stability, and in the United States in the 1950s this was exacerbated as the confidence of the immediate postwar years gave way to the Cold War and the perceived threat of Communism. These factors manifested, among other things, in a strict unwritten dress code, and garments designed to reinforce the mass values of capitalism and the image of a society in control of itself. These were epitomized by the gray flannel suit and other forms of prescriptive clothing for men, and also for women – including the girdle. As Mary Douglas showed in *Natural Symbols* (1996: xxxv), the more value people set on social constraints, the more value they set on symbols of bodily control. Adding gender to this model, the ritualization of dress in 1950s America can be seen as a materialization of the desire to reinforce polarized gender roles, as an aspect of control in the face of change, and in support of the cult of family and 'normality' which always arises in postwar periods.

Another approach is through feminist anthropology and women's studies which promote female autonomy, in which the girdle can be seen primarily as an instrument of patriarchal oppression. Veblen (1953) was an early exponent of this view, describing the corset as a mutilation that transformed women into chattels, economically dependent on men. There is also the question of sexuality, how and by whom it is constructed, and its relationship to social control, issues raised originally by Foucault. In this paradigm, the girdle can be seen as the ultimate instrument of social, physical and sexual control, the garment that defined domination and the dominated. In addition there is an extensive critical literature on how women's bodies have been commodified, standardized and controlled in various ways, how women became alienated from their own bodies and bodily processes, how ideologies of 'health' and 'beauty' enforce social control, and how images and expectations of women's bodies have, under late capitalism, become inextricably entangled with economic and social processes (Lakoff and Scherr 1984; Locke 1993a, 1993b, 1999; Martin 1994; Nader 1997). From all perspectives, girdle-wearing was essential. The complex 'need' for a girdle is the kind of taken-for-granted understanding, an implicit but obligatory value in material form, that made the foundation market so attractive to Dupont.

The cultural biography of Lycra presented here touches on all of these approaches and provides material for future analyses within them and in other fields. However, in following the ethnographic moment, it takes a broader, less explicitly political perspective. Instead, the biography focuses on how one of America's largest and most powerful corporations once saw women, how that changed over time, and how these changes influenced the stuff they produced or didn't produce. Lycra offers unique insights into the process because it came to the market on the cusp of a major social transformation with which it became entangled, and because it came to have a defining relationship with the Boomer cohort for which it had been created. As a fiber, Lycra adds another dimension to the study of stuff. As will be seen in Chapter 5, the very materiality of Lycra – the sensuous and completely new physical sensations conveyed by 'stretch' – resonated with revolutionary bodily attitudes and values that emerged among the Boomer cohort during a major moment of social change.

Dupont, the Girdle and the Search for Stretch

Dupont first came to grips with the girdle through an uncharacteristically small-scale application. Boned and laced corsets had long been in use, but by the 1930s 'rubberized' alternatives made from rubber-covered thread were becoming widely used, the transition concealed by the fact that they were socially invisible, worn under clothes. Rubberized foundations were more conducive than boned and laced corsets to the smooth, simple, and slender clothing silhouettes that were coming into vogue. The 1930s also saw the beginning of what proved to be a continuing mania for dieting. Staying slender and youthful were now seen as a woman's duty, and for those who had not been successful with diets, one alternative was the reducing corset.

These garments were made of rubber molded onto silk and then perfo-rated, allowing the skin to breathe while at the same time stimulating perspira-tion which would lead to weight loss. Attracted by their popularity and potential profitability, Dupont entered the reducing corset market in coopera-tion with a manufacturer in 1936, announcing its new venture as follows:

> At present there is an unprecedented world-wide swing to the use of rubber in corsets. Just recently Fifth Avenue shops in New York City advertised cor-sets made of perforated rubber imported from England and priced at more than twenty dollars. The Paris corsetiere has long known the advantage of rubber as a reducing agent and also as a material for foundation garments. Parisian importations are being sold at prices ranging from ten to fifty dol-lars. So now American women who choose this common sense and prac-tical way of reducing will be able to buy, for as little as five dollars, a Diana reducing corset. That garments of this kind are in demand is clearly indi-cated by the following experience. R.H. Macy & Co of New York, carrying a store-wide promotion behind the Diana line, sold thousands of dollars worth of garments in the first day and a half of its sale, and on Tuesday afternoon, following the appearance of an advertisement in the *New York Times*, had completely sold out of its stock and was wildly clamouring for more. The development of an improved line of reducing corsets will be something new to many women and particularly those who have watched with concern and finally dismay the poundage mount, Hollywood diet, spinach and other experiments to the contrary. Perhaps the shattering of an atom with a crackling stream of blue fire will be of practical significance to posterity … but the woman who is able through the use of du Pont Per-forated Health Rubber to keep her youthful figure might consider these products even more essential to their happiness and well being.[21]

The appearance and popularity of the reducing corset signaled the emergence of a new concept of the 'ideal' woman's figure and new ideas about female health, bespeaking a shift in cultural values or ideologies, unremarked at the time. It was a perfect example of a dynamic described by Sahlins (1976: 185):

> because it appears to the producers as a quest for pecuniary gain and to the consumer as an acquisition of useful goods, the basic symbolic char-acter of the process goes on behind the back of the participants, and usu-ally the economists as well.

The success of the Diana reducing corset confirmed for Dupont the possib-ilities in less specialized applications. Through the work done on rubber and on solvents in other Dupont divisions, the company was aware of the short-comings of natural rubber when used in undergarments, the main drawbacks being the tendency to deteriorate after contact with sweat, body oils or detergents, and when exposed to sunlight. The potential market for a producer who could devise a superior stretch fiber made of synthetic rubber to use in foundation garments was enormous, and in casting around for new needs to fill, nothing could have seemed more certain to Dupont than the girdle.

'Resilience', it will be remembered, had emerged as a desirable fiber quality in marketing research – a vague term that then had to be given material form in the laboratories. Now the same approach was applied to a different fiber quality – 'stretch'. As laboratory work on nylon continued through World War II, the company thought it had found a candidate for development in an elastic nylon fiber they called '0-5', and began trials. As with their other fibers, trials involved getting mills to make the fabric, which was then passed to foundation manufacturers to make sample garments that were then subjected to wear-tests. The initial results were disappointing but, in 1946, as soon as the war was over, the Development Department decided to press ahead, sending the following memorandum to Pioneering Research, instructing them to resume developing a fiber that could be used in a high-prestige elastic yarn.[22]

The specific objective was girdles. Following established procedure, Dupont had undertaken market research, which revealed a promising opening:

> There is believed to be a gap in available underwear between the girdle, which is too cumbersome and boardy for most trim figures and the knit panty, which fits snugly but applies no pressure. All merchandisers with whom we have discussed the subject agree that a large market should exist … we should begin now a new and somewhat accelerated phase of the work.[23]

These findings were handed on to the scientists in the Research Department, but fiber 0-5 continued to be problematic. Apart from difficulties with the fiber itself, performance requirements for foundation wear turned out to be more demanding than anticipated, and the dynamics of stretch as tested in the laboratory did not correspond to those generated when tested on a body. In addition, the wear-testers drew attention to factors that anthropologists would recognize as 'cultural', and which the scientists hadn't taken into account: there was a slight tendency to discoloration which the women didn't like even though the garment was not going to be seen in public, and they were worried that they might not be able to iron the girdle, even though girdles were not normally ironed. Ironing practically everything was then considered obligatory, the sign of good housewifeliness, a cultural attitude that

Dupont would battle on another front with its wash-and-wear fibers. Despite intensive work on the new elastic fiber, success with 0-5 remained elusive. Meanwhile, as the population expanded demographically with the continuing baby boom, the potential market for girdles grew.

In 1952, an internal memorandum circulated in the Textile Fibers Division that throws important light on the market considerations and pressures that shaped elastic fiber development at Dupont. The company, it noted, had traditionally manufactured products 'which do a premium job at a premium price'. A premium elastic fiber was an ideal research goal, and the scientists were urged to 'have some specific product under development within the next year or so'.[24]

By 1954, with no finalized girdle fiber in sight, corporate exasperation was running high, as shown in this memorandum from the Development Department to Pioneering Research (below). Also clear are the tensions between the perceived perfectionism of Research and the pragmatism of Development. Further evidence of these tensions can be found in the comments I found on the memo, written in the margin by an anonymous member of the Pioneering Research team. The memo is quoted here at length because it led directly to the birth of Lycra, and the hand-written comments are shown in bold, underlined.

Displacement of rubber from present end uses. We have been knocking on this door for more than ten years. It is the number one objective because chances appear good for moving into parts of this market in a straightforward manner relatively fast – within the next two years. We should not put off moving in this direction until we have a 'perfect' product, or even the best one that might ultimately be found. We should not hold out for one which will displace rubber in all of its present end uses. There is no 'perfect' product because no one yarn will satisfy all elastic end-use requirements.

The thing to do is to pick a product now which is attractive from the standpoint of raw materials, availability and price, manufacturing process and properties needed for the bulk of the elastic yarn uses and make it commercial as quickly as possible. It is extremely desirable to be the first to get into the field with a reasonably satisfactory product.

End uses to go after first. The bulk of the rubber yarns used now are in the following end uses: foundation garments; brassieres; suspenders and garters; sock tops; surgical hosiery; elastic bandages; swimsuits. Attention should be concentrated on these few end uses, plus hosiery afterwelts, avoiding the necessity for spreading the justifiable effort thinly over a wide variety of potential end uses. With this situation, a lot can be accomplished market-development-wise in a short time by a few people working intensively with only a few customers. (**So?**)

End uses for new elastic fibers. This area of work could well be the most important aspect of the new elastic fibers. (**It already is**) One example is the blending of staple elastic and non-elastic fibers for new kinds of spun fabrics and end uses. However, it necessarily requires more time and a different kind of program to put over this kind of development than that discussed above. More time and research will be needed to determine what kind of fiber properties are best for, as yet, undefined or meagerly characterized end-uses.

Moving the trade to new fibers for new end uses is a slower and more cumbersome operation than getting them to substitute a similar, but better or cheaper, product for the one they are now using in well-established end-products. This objective may merit large research programs, conceivably larger than for the rubber yarn replacement work. These two programs should, however, be kept separate and distinct from each other as far as their objectives, tempo and scope of exploitation are concerned.

Within two weeks (**star-gazing**) you should know how you would want to make the first candidate as close to these properties as possible, within another month to six weeks thereafter. (**Better get a magician on the pay-roll**)[25]

Girdles were now designated as the primary 'desired goal product' and a promising new fiber called 'Fiber K', later trademarked as Lycra, was selected as the new best candidate for development. There was no 'Eureka moment' for Lycra, no sudden and dramatic discovery in the laboratory, as there had been with nylon, when a filament grown in a beaker at Pioneering Research became the textile equivalent of Lister's discovery of penicillin mold growing in a Petri dish. Lycra was the result of slow and painstaking work on polymer technology which had gone on for many years, and would continue for many more. Dupont now went into action on several fronts. Within days of the memorandum, a patent-filing program was implemented. Pioneering Research had to prepare two variants of the final patent that would protect Lycra against piracy – a short version called the 'Optimistic Approach' and a longer version known as 'The Fate Worse Than Death' option.[26] On January 31, 1955, chemist Joe Shivers of Pioneering Research filed Dupont's patent applications for elastic copolymers and fibers. Lycra had been born.

4

LAUNCHING LYCRA

Twenty years had gone by since Dupont first became interested in stretch fibers, and although the company had yet to successfully enter the mainstream foundation market, that market had remained remarkably stable in both America and Britain. As the postwar recovery in Europe proceeded, Dupont and the large foundation manufacturers – the major customers for Dupont's undergarment fibers – extended their fiber, fabric and garment operations overseas, beginning in Britain where they were delighted to discover that, as in America, women considered the wearing of girdles obligatory. For girls on both sides of the Atlantic, donning the girdle for the first time was a kind of rite of passage, a sign of transition from girlhood to womanhood, just as assuming corsets and putting up the hair instead of wearing it long had been in a previous era. This was a time when little girls were considered to be junior versions of their mothers, a period when women's magazines carried patterns of mother-and-daughter outfits, while Dupont sponsored mother and daughter fashion shows, and ran advertisements showing mothers and daughters in matching outfits. Women wanted to look 'youthful' and girls wanted to be 'grown up'; girdles were essential for both.

The girls of the 1950s were not the independent consumers and shoppers they are now, nor were they able to influence parental purchases to the extent that they do today, so their profile remained indistinct to producers who saw them indirectly, through their mothers. Mothers were the prime movers in first girdle purchases, taking their daughters to the store where they bought their own girdles, and entrusting them to their own accustomed saleslady or fitter. When self-service became the rule, mothers tended to select girdles in appropriate styles for their daughter that were made by the same manufacturer who made their own. Not to get one's daughter 'properly' girdled in this way would been seen – as more than one woman put it to me explicitly – to have failed in one's duty as a mother. As twenty years previously, mothers and daughters of the 1950s found themselves in the embrace of an industry whose presence in their lives was unquestioned, and whose advertisements whispered to them in a special language which described girdles as 'considerate', 'stream-

Figure 4.1 Mother and Daughter: Orlon Good-Looking Clothes, courtesy of Hagley Museum and Library.

lining', 'quicker than a diet', 'glamorous', 'very necessary' and 'the foundation of good form'. Leading manufacturers such as Playtex had their girdles endorsed by top designers of the day like Christian Dior, and girdles were so taken for granted that early Barbie dolls – the first 'grown-up' dolls with contemporary fashion wardrobes, introduced in 1959 – were sold provided with girdles.

As the 1950s drew to a close, there was a buoyant mood of general optimism. American business saw the coming decade as 'The Big Sixties', a time of onrushing opportunity that promised to be 'a decade of unparalleled prosperity, of record growth, of extraordinary improvement in incomes and living standards, of expansion in domestic and foreign markets'.[1] It was foreseen that as purchasing power rose and leisure time increased, 'giant markets of the future will flourish in a world of abundance', with 25 percent more consumers in the population by 1970. It was in this positive atmosphere of cultural and commercial certainty that Dupont moved on to launch the new stretch fiber and girdles made of it. All the different elements, operations and procedures that had been developed in the Textile Fibers Division over many years were mobilized, and the new fiber received the full treatment. The first stage was large-scale trade evaluation. Warner's, Vanity Fair and other major manufacturers who had participated in the unsuccessful trial of fiber 0-5 were invited to join in trials of the new fiber. All accepted, and agreed to be supplied with sample fiber to make up into girdles for testing under conditions of the greatest secrecy.

Brainstorming

To stimulate corporate thinking about the future development of the new fiber while the trials were underway, Dupont held a 'brainstorming' session. 'Creativity' was the business buzzword of the 1950s, and brainstorming was a technique developed by Alex Osborn of Barton, Batten, Durstine and Osborn (BBDO), an advertising agency that worked with Dupont over many years. In Osborn's words, 'brainstorming means using the brain to storm a creative problem, and to do so in commando fashion, with each "stormer" audaciously attacking the same objective'.[2] In its heyday, brainstorming was used by many of the major American companies, including Campbell's Soups, Eastman Kodak and Sheraton Hotels, who applied it to problems in the areas of sales, merchandising, promotion, packaging, cost reduction and product use and adaptation. Group dynamics – the ideal number was 12-to-14 persons – were central to brainstorming. The atmosphere was meant to be lively and intense: the wilder and more unorthodox the ideas, the better. Brainstormers were encouraged to 'hitchhike' or improve on the suggestions of other group members. In some companies, hitchhikers were required to jump to their feet and click their fingers to indicate that they were about to 'hitch'. Suggestions were recorded by a stenographer verbatim, without identification as to the source, screened then passed on to the research, technical or sales department, or any other relevant party. At its height, brainstorming sessions were held twice a week at Dupont, covering products and problems in all divisions. The company even brainstormed on the term 'brainstorm', considering whether an alternative name might be better. 'Skull session', 'cranial conjugation' and 'Du Pont idea plotting' were suggested: 'brainstorming' was retained.

For the new fiber, the brainstorm problem was – what possible applications can you see for stretch yarn? The session produced a large number of suggestions, apart from the obvious use in foundation garments. Some – such as *tonneau* covers for sports cars, football jerseys, one-size clothes, changeable helmet covers for military camouflage purposes, stretch dresses, suits and pillow covers – have come into daily use. Others – dining room seat covers with a Christmas motif (to give a room a quick and easy holiday look); can covers (to make beer cans more attractive); chin straps (beauty aids for double chins) and asparagus holders (tubes to slip over bunches of asparagus spears to keep them intact during cooking) have not. Significantly – the postwar 'baby boom' being well underway – many of the suggestions referred to children. Among them were stretchy covers for school books, expanding toy bags (to keep children's rooms neat), doll clothes (to fit any size doll), crib covers, baby bottle holders, baby harnesses, baby carriage covers and children's costumes (Halloween and fancy dress costumes that would stretch over the years, making the initial purchases more economical).[3]

Dupont now gave the new fiber the trademark name 'Lycra', selected according to established practice from a number of possible names generated within the company, an indication that the fiber was beginning to acquire an identity. Initially, this identity was a purely internal one. Until Dupont was ready to supply the mass market, Lycra would be concealed under a blanket of secrecy.

Sampling and wear-testing, the next stage in commercializing any fiber, always presented Dupont with the challenge of supplying enough fiber for testing before special machinery designed to work with the new fiber had been perfected or factories had been organized to produce it on any scale. There are many apocryphal stories about the lengths to which Dupont employees went to preserve secrecy while transferring fiber samples. These small batches of sampling fiber were then made up into girdles for highly confidential wear-testing. Different companies had different testing procedures, but all were exhaustive. One involved a test panel composed of a designer and 100 employees who wear-tested all items. During a test cycle of two weeks, each garment was examined three times every day, washed after each wearing, and then examined before the next wearing.[4] Another firm commissioned a research organization to carry out wear-tests of staggering complexity: sixty-nine women received a Lycra girdle, another sixty-nine a rubber core girdle in the same style as a control, twenty-nine women received a Lycra panty girdle and another twenty-nine a rubber core panty girdle as a control. The girdles had been carefully matched in weight and appearance, so it was difficult to tell them apart. The women testers were also matched in terms of household income, age, marital status and other factors, so similar women wore similar types of girdle. This intensive wear-test went on for eight months[5] while the designs and the fiber were refined and perfected.

On the morning of October 28, 1959, the world's fashion and trade press, along with leading manufacturers of foundation garments, textiles and clothing, gathered at the Empire State Building on Fifth Avenue in New York City. Dominating the street synonymous with American style, the skyscraper symbolized American commercial supremacy, housing the offices of many top corporations, including Dupont, who had summoned press and producers to the announcement of its newest textile fiber. Rumors of this new development had swept the textile and garment industries, and excitement was keen as key members of the Textile Fibers Division delivered their presentation. Lycra, they revealed, was an elastomeric fiber that stretched and snapped back into place like rubber, but unlike rubber was resistant to deterioration caused by perspiration, cosmetic oils and lotions. It could be dyed, machine washed and machine dried. Although Lycra was much lighter than rubberized elastic thread, it had two-to-three-times as much restraining power, and would be used to make girdles that were light, soft and sheer while providing the same figure control provided by bulkier foundations. Expectations for the new fiber ran high, and the *Wilmington Morning News* ran a banner headline:[6]

New Du Pont Fiber Could 'Girdle' World – One Day.

Dupont hoped that Lycra would bring about as great a change in the women's foundation garment industry as nylon had in the hosiery industry. And it did, although it is doubtful if anyone in that room on the day that Lycra was launched could have foreseen quite how that would come about.

From White Collar to Blue Collar

The focus now switches from a white-collar context of scientific and marketing research to the blue-collar context of the factories where the new fiber would be produced. Standard business and labor studies tend to focus on management *or* workers, rarely both, unless examining conflict between them. In a

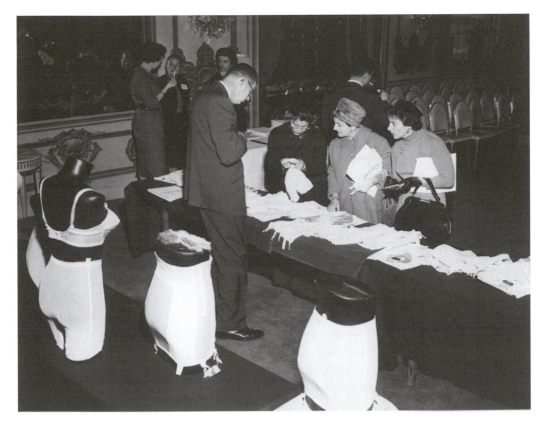

Figure 4.2 Women examining sample girdles at the press launch of Lycra in 1959, courtesy of Hagley Museum and Library.

company like Dupont, with a paternalistic tradition of mutuality, strong company culture and a remarkable archive, it is possible to construct a more nuanced cultural account of production than is generally possible. This in turn provides insight into the meanings that a product – in this case the fiber Lycra and girdles made of it – come to have for the people who make them, and how a product can act as a unifying focus within a company.

From the beginning of its textile operations, Dupont had set up factories to produce each of their fibers, and these factories with their attendant communities of workers, often living in company housing with several or all members of a family employed by Dupont, embodied much of the spirit and ethos of the original powder works on the Brandywine. The life of the Dupont fiber factories of the period can be traced through company and employee magazines, sources that have received little academic attention to date – a striking lacuna in light of their importance as a record of the way stuff comes into being. Citing their origins in the period of national anti-business sentiment at the start of the twentieth century, Marchand sees all company and employee magazines largely as cynical attempts by corporate employers to promote company values, prime among them competition and the virtues of free enterprise; to motivate workers and boost their morale and productivity; to substitute a paper community for face-to-face work relations; and to re-establish 'a direct line between the men at the big desks and the workers and families in their homes' (Marchand 1998: 108). Above all, in his view, company magazines were intended to establish and continually reinforce the notion of the 'big family', the corporate family, thus humanizing big business. But do company magazines construct the communities they describe, or reflect them? Marchand and others (Brandes 1976) emphasize the former, and from this has followed the general tendency to assume that the descriptions contained in magazines have little independent validity, and therefore to disregard them as sources of information. However – depending on the magazines and the companies – these publications can equally be seen as a detailed and unique record of working communities dedicated in a highly focused way to the pro-duction of particular consumer goods. Company magazines are company towns on paper, and as such are highly suitable for anthropological investiga-tion. Indeed, it is precisely *because* they are meant to be constructing that they become valuable as a site where the producers' views are stated explicitly. Further, in the case of Dupont, company culture was not something foisted upon the workers from outside; it had been embedded in every aspect of the company from its beginnings, linking the physiocratic principles of free trade and enterprise and the belief in scientific research to the notion of 'family', with one significant difference. Many company magazines addressed their readership as members of 'the American Sugar family', the 'RCA family', or 'the Ford family', in the latter case referring to the automobile workers in the Ford plants, not the descendants of the founder, Henry Ford. Dupont had three kinds of company magazine – the corporate *Dupont Magazine,* the employee magazine *Better Living* and magazines such as *Fiber Facts* which were produced for particular Dupont works or factories, but none of them mention the 'Dupont family' of workers. There was only one du Pont family. Everyone who worked for Dupont, on any site and at any level, blue collar or white collar, was known as a 'Duponter'.

Waynesboro and the Mass Production of Lycra

Even as Lycra went public, its availability was outstripped by demand, and on the same day that Lycra was launched in New York, Dupont announced the opening of a multi-million-dollar Lycra fiber production unit at Waynesboro, Virginia, where Lycra fiber would be produced for the whole of the country. Dupont had opened a rayon manufacturing plant in Waynesboro in 1928, later shifting the main production of the works to Orlon. Bringing the new fiber to Waynesboro was seen as further guaranteeing the future of the community, so even before production began, Lycra was received with enthusiasm. *Fiber Facts* was the magazine published by Dupont for the Waynesboro Works. The same surnames appear again and again in different departments; husbands, wives, aunts, uncles, sons and daughters, some in the third generation of employment at this Dupont factory. Issues of *Fiber Facts* from the early 1960s reveal the reassuring and nostalgic world of small-town America, and a close-knit community who shared a life of prideful work and the wholesome play of baseball games, soapbox derbies, bowling and movies like *She Wore A Yellow Ribbon* starring John Wayne down at the Waynesboro Theater. And where every woman, young or old, wore a girdle.

The important role played by works like Waynesboro and the technical experts and engineers based there are often overlooked in studies of the production and consumption of stuff, but they are an essential part of the commercialization process. As one Dupont employee put it: 'Research is one field and manufacturing is another, and somewhere there has to be a link between the two.'[7] Waynesboro was that link. The Waynesboro documents also reveal another overlooked contrast, between the valorized scientists at Pioneering Research and the largely unsung technical engineers at Waynesboro. Ironically, it was often the engineers, more familiar with the practical aspects of the fiber, who had a better idea of its potential than the scientists. As a former Dupont research scientist told me:

> In the early days, no one thought Lycra would go as far as it has. But one guy did, he saw it coming, all the ways Lycra could be used, not just in underwear. He talked about it *all the time*. But to begin with, no one listened to him, because he was 'just an engineer'.

This passage from *Fiber Facts* shows how the Waynesboro engineers saw their role and their importance to the overall scheme of things, coupled to a reminder from the company about the ultimate objective:

> There is a long road to travel and pay for before an 'experiment' comes to life in the form of a new product. It has been said of twenty full scale laboratory experiments, one fulfils the hope of the chemist. In other words, for every successful idea that comes out of a test tube, there are nineteen others that have not proved out, ideas that for some reason or another have failed to show enough potential to merit continued study. But after the Research lab has uncovered an idea, a new product or a new fiber, they turn their know-how over to the Technical section, which translates their research material into a workable plant process. The function of

Research then is to search out and uncover new ideas and products, not to develop them on a plant scale. Our plant technical section closes the gap between research and the plant process. It translates what Research has come up with into plant processes and equipment. Their main jobs are to stay ahead of competition, to improve the overall quality picture, to look critically at equipment and raw materials, and to develop new end uses that will keep our product first. Technical must evaluate too the chances Du Pont has of coming up with a profit. If research, technical and manufacturing costs prove too high, the product cannot sell at an attractive enough cost to be successful. We must remember that our reason for being here is to make a profit.[8]

The process of improvement was ongoing, a distinctive feature of the Dupont system since the powder-making days. Though costly, it made commercial sense. First, new processes gave Dupont's customers a competitive edge, and also made the Dupont salesman's job easier. As one Dupont Orlon salesman remembered, 'Every six months, Dupont came out with something new and better, a whiter shade, a stronger fiber, a better product.'[9] Second, new processes that could be patented protected and strengthened the company's commercial and legal positions. Third, to the consumer, 'new and better' would, hopefully, render 'old' as 'obsolete', leading to new purchases and greater profits. Ongoing improvement and innovation were the way Dupont was able to maintain its market leadership and continue its traditional practice of 'manufacturing products that do a premium job at premium prices'.[10]

Two paired themes – the valorization of work and of profit – resonate in *Fiber Facts*, where Lycra is presented as the source of profit, and also as the embodiment of fundamental beliefs and a way of life. Here, profit itself is not just a matter of money, but of morality; it becomes a value beyond price, the engine that drives innovation and supports the local community. What resonates also is the argument for big business, a reaffirmation of the company's position, couched in terms little changed since the 1920s, and repeating the identification with the nation that had always been part of the company's public stance:

Without getting into a political debate, we'd like to defend the theory that 'what's good for General Motors *is* good for America'. *Fiber Facts* is sick to death of the stigma industry has inherited with regard to 'profit'. What paid for the $10 million in research and development for Lycra if it wasn't profit? Profit is the lifeblood that pays taxes to support the government, yet industrial leaders are 'tainted' by this profit, as if they were dishonest. So let's get it straight. We've built a plant to manufacture Lycra in hopes of making an honest buck. And if profit is a dirty word, then we should have our mouths washed out with soap. We're proud of being 'BIG'. There is a need for 'bigness' in our economy today. Who but a big company could afford to invest $10 million on an untried spandex fiber? Who but a big company could dare risk the chance of a failure?... So we are proud that our bigness paid out $18 million dollars at Waynesboro Works last year. We are proud too that the thousands of firms who supply us with raw materials were able to offer employment to thousands of other people. So when anyone points a finger at Du Pont for being big, throw your chests out and say – 'Sure we are big and we are helping the American economy grow big too.'[11]

Fiber Facts showed employees in all departments and sometimes members of their families producing and wear-testing Lycra and the new Lycra variants currently in development. Bobby, the son of a technical laboratory employee and quarterback on the town's high-school football team, posed in experimental football pants of nylon and Lycra. The pretty daughter of a maintenance employee, a local beauty contest entrant, received the company gift of a Rose Marie Reid swimsuit with Lycra to wear in the swimsuit section of the beauty competition. Eighty female employees wear-tested nylon and Lycra support hose and later Betty, Edna, Alma, Gladys, Ruby and their friends sat for a commemorative photograph, stockinged legs proudly outstretched before them. Theresa, a glamorous works stenographer, gamely posed outdoors in a swimsuit for publicity purposes even as Waynesboro was digging out of an eleven-inch snowfall.

Each issue of *Fiber Facts* contained a mixture of articles of male or female interest, exemplifying gendered meaning. Those aimed at male employees were couched in terms of competition:

The Product Superintendant for Lycra said this week, 'It is up to us all to keep Du Pont out in front. In the new field of spandex fibers there are already eight known firms either in production or seriously working on developing. Du Pont is the "guy out front" at the moment, but breathing down our necks are a lot of tough competitors. How do we stay out in front in this tough race? Quality, service, cost, new deniers [yarn types], anything that will make Lycra run better in the customers' mills.'[12]

Women's articles, by contrast, had a more personal angle. Ladies were told, 'Forget the diet and buy yourself a Lycra foundation garment!'[13] Just before the formal opening of the Lycra unit at Waynesboro, there was a Saturday night 'start-up dance' at the works recreation center, built by Dupont for the employees in 1939. There was live music by the Esquires, and a special incentive for the ladies: the first fifty to arrive at the dance wearing a foundation garment of Lycra would receive a small corsage, and two girdles of Lycra were given as draw prizes during the evening.

Everyone at the dance would have been well aware of how the prize girdles had been made. Just as *Fiber Facts* kept different departments in the works up

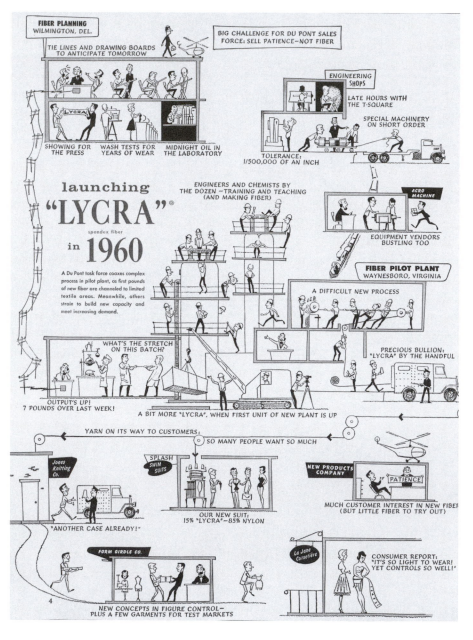

Figure 4.3 Launching 'Lycra' in 1960, courtesy of Hagley Museum and Library.

to date with each others' activities, so they kept employees informed of what happened to the fiber when it left Waynesboro, emphasizing that 'yarn quality here means fabric quality in customers' mills'. The links between Waynesboro and the wider fiber world were often presented in the form of 'picture stories'. One told the frame-by-frame story of the making of a Warner's girdle of Lycra, illustrated with photographs of Waynesboro and Warner's employees. The cones of Lycra yarn were spun and checked for quality at Waynesboro, then sent to Warner's Weaving and Finishing Plant in Rhode Island, where they were unpacked in the presence of a Dupont technical representative, wound onto a knitting beam, and run through the machine under the eye of a Dupont specialist. The finished fabric was checked by Warner and Dupont inspectors, cut into panels, embroidered, gartered, stitched together, boxed and ended up in downtown Wilmington, Dupont's home city, as girdles on sale at Leggett's department store. For Waynesboro, this was the meaningful commodity chain, but it was just a segment in Dupont's larger fiber chain, the company's own representation of which is shown in the diagrammatic *Launching 'Lycra' in 1960*.[14]

This is basically a production model, without the cultural elements – the history, the corporate culture, the marketing of Lycra and the people it was made for and sold to – all of which are essential to understanding how stuff comes into being, enters our lives and comes to have meaning for us. As *Fiber Facts* put it – 'marketing picks Lycra up where the plant leaves off',[15] and it is to marketing that we now turn.

Marketing Lycra

Dupont launched Lycra with what, for them, was an unprecedented publicity campaign, taking advertisements in newspapers and full-page ads in leading women's magazines such as *Vogue*, *Harpers Bazaar*, *Glamour*, *Mademoiselle*, *McCall's*, *Ladies Home Journal* and *Good Housekeeping*. The theme of one of the advertisement campaigns, which featured close-ups of girdles labeled with the captions below, was 'at last', which gives considerable insight into the experience of girdle wearing:[16]

At last, a girdle that lets you golf, bowl, ski – do any sport in utter comfort!

At last, a girdle that lets you breathe – even after shrimp, steak, French fries, parfait and coffee!

At last, a girdle that controls so effortlessly, you'll feel like size 10 again!

At last, a girdle that lets you put in an 8-hour day – controlled but comfortable!

At last, a girdle with such comfortable control – you'll scarcely know you're wearing it!

These ads were meant to appeal directly to consumers, but were also a 'service' to Dupont's customers and customers' customers, who the company reminded to 'stock, promote and advertise foundations containing "Lycra" to take advantage of the strong, clear selling story these Du Pont ads will be telling *your* customers in every season of the big year ahead!'[17]

Dupont's customers also joined in the promotion initiative. Warner's, a major foundation company which had participated in the early Lycra wear-tests, took twenty-eight full pages of national advertising in ten national women's magazines on their own account to publicize their girdles with Lycra, and many of Dupont's other customers doubled their advertising budget to advertise their use of Lycra.[18]

Lycra Retail Marketing

The degree of stretch that Lycra fiber gave to garments made with it was unprecedented. Because Lycra was unlike any existing fiber – in the same way that rayon, nylon and wash-and-wear fabrics were unique when they were launched – Dupont had to mount an intensive campaign to teach staff how to sell foundation garments made of Lycra, and to show consumers how to wear them. The promotional materials produced by the company for these purposes give insights into the way people thought about bodies (and other people's bodies), and how the invention and introduction of a new fiber obliged them to think about bodies in new ways. Because it is ephemeral and the relatively small proportion of examples that have survived are not easily accessible, retail sales material has not figured in the academic literature to date, despite its centrality to the mediation between production and consumption. The material presented here therefore makes a contribution to an overlooked aspect of the field, and gives insights into the challenges faced by producers when trying to sell a new kind of materiality, and also shows how producers used the 'rules' to construct consumers.

Dupont provided retail sales staff with booklets entitled:[19]

How to Promote 'Lycra' Spandex Figures – and Have Better Sales Figures Too!

Selling Tips – How to Make 'Lycra' Spandex Fiber E-x-p-a-n-d Your Sales

How to Make Your Figures Add Up with Proper Bras and Girdles

One began, 'The great thing about "Lycra" for you is that every woman who wears a girdle and bra (and isn't that practically every one?) is a potential customer for Lycra.' Another booklet gave a list of common customer questions and problems, to which the salesperson was encouraged to respond by suggesting a foundation garment in Lycra:

Have you got a nice, comfortable girdle that will take three inches off my hips?

The last girdle I bought was fine for standing … but for sitting down …

Why do my foundations lose their shape and, after a while, take on my shape?

Don't you have a girdle I can eat a full course meal in without feeling bound around the middle?[20]

A Dupont cartoon-style booklet, an illustrated primer on good sales technique, recounted *The Adventures of Selma the Star Sales Girl* [21] and her winning ways of explaining to customers that girdles with Lycra were light in weight, softer and more comfortable, easy to wash and long-wearing. Another booklet presented retail staff with different categories of figure types, matched up to what they needed in the way of girdles and bras: 'Well-Rounded – you'd like less of you' and 'Under-endowed – you'd like to equalize'. The *Selling Tips* booklet concluded with these warnings for owners of new girdles with Lycra: 'Never pull a girdle with tips of fingers (palms only)', 'Never clutch a girdle at the top' and 'Never yank the bottom down'.

Lycra Press Releases

Company-generated press releases were the source of many of the 'feature' stories on Lycra that appeared in national, syndicated and local newspapers, and were a major element in Dupont's consumer-oriented promotion of Lycra. As in all companies, releases are sent out in the hopes that journalists will pick up the stories and use or 'feature' them in some way, thereby generating free publicity for the company and product by presenting what is essentially commercial product information in the guise of non-commercial 'news' or 'editorial' material. The quality of press releases is variable, depending on the writer and on the newsworthiness of the product, but at their best they can be highly effective, conveying to the journalists' audience information that requires no exertion on the part of the journalists, who can pass the press releases off, more or less verbatim, as their own work

– a form of plagiarism that, for once, is acceptable to the issuing company or agency.

At Dupont, these press packs often included sketches or photographs of the product that could be reproduced free of charge. Releases were written in a range of styles, from fashion-journalese to consumer-informative depending on the publications they were sent to, timed as far as possible to coincide with publishing schedules – swimsuit releases, for example, are frequently issued in December, to catch the holiday/swimsuit/travel features that traditionally appear from January to March. Dupont's Lycra press releases were compiled from market-research information, sales reports, retail trend information, fashion forecasts and even company brainstorming sessions. Here are two representative examples which reflect the twin foci of the Textile Fibers Division – fashion/style and function/utility – and show how stuff conveys cultural meanings and values:

<u>Fashion Press Release</u>

Good News! Girls are going to look like girls again as Paris stylists have put the figure back in style. While the return of shape is not limited to one fixed silhouette, the trend is toward a slim, close-to-the-body line with three fashion points in common: a high bosom; fitted sometimes even skin-tight midriff, and smoothed-down hips. As Paris goes, so goes Seventh Avenue, all of which means that feminine curves are due for a big revival on this side of the Atlantic too. Women who for years managed to hide some of their problems under fluid, 'relaxed' clothes now will find it necessary to correct the problems with the *right foundation garments.* The relation of inner-shape to outer-shape is such a vital part of current fashion thinking that one French designer opened the showing of his collection with a corselet and it has been said that his firm will not sell a dress without a companion undergarment. One of the quickest ways to acquire the trim specifications called for in both Paris originals and their American copies is with 'Lycra' spandex fiber which brings to foundation garments a unique combination of lightweight comfort and control plus the softness and suppleness that the fashion's scheme of things demands.... The charm of the clothes depends on corsetry with an uncorseted look – in other words, firm but gentle shaping. And this is exactly what Lycra provides.... Here's a quick run-down on just a few of the styles available in Lycra and how they pertain to fashion: high top girdles to raise the waistline and carve a concave midriff ... long-line bras for a youthful, lifted bustline and sculptured mid-section ... panties and girdles with reinforced side panels to pare inches off the hips ... long-leg panties for smoothness both over and below the hips ... all-in-one garments for a long, molded torso ... strapless brassalieres and torsolettes to accentuate the waistlines of cocktail and evening costumes.[22]

Function Press Release

New Foundations with 'Lycra' Solve Weighty Problems. This year may well go down in fashion history as the year that brought the final emancipation of women from the rib-crushing restraints of rigid corsetry. The era of free and easy figure control, which came into sight with the development of 'Lycra' spandex fiber, has arrived at last for all women. Even majestic matrons can now take a light and comfortable approach to weighty problems. In fact, some of the biggest undercover news for fall centers on garments powered by 'Lycra' that are designed for women of generous proportions. Until recently, foundations made with this unique elastic textile fiber were aimed mainly at average and junior figures. Now for the first time, women who either need or want maximum control have a variety of styles from which to choose. The manufacture of such garments has been made possible by the introduction of stronger yarns of 'Lycra'. What more could a woman ask?[23]

In the biographical process envisioned by Kopytoff (1986), Lycra had now taken on several meanings. In its chemical birth as the seventh member of Dupont's family of fibers, Lycra embodied the traditions of family and firm. Its subsequent development reflected and perpetuated Dupont's corporate culture and practices. The investment in time and money that brought it into being was emblematic of the values of free enterprise and capitalism, a validation of what the company saw as its heroic and historic mission. For Dupont's scientists, Lycra confirmed the wisdom of pure research, while for Dupont's engineers it affirmed the importance of technological expertise. For the Waynesboro workers, Lycra had ensured their way of life and reinforced their everyday values, while for Dupont, Dupont's customers and customer's customers, Lycra had provided a livelihood. To the consumer, Lycra was presented as a fiber of modernity, facilitating the 'new' modern way of life, and creating the ideal body. The irony of subjecting this most innovative of fibers to the most traditional of uses in the form of the girdle, passed unnoticed. Lycra now moves along the trajectory, to assume new meanings – none of them foreseen by producers or Lycra's first consumers.

The Boomers

The Dupont principle of premium goods at premium prices held firm, and the demand for girdles of Lycra outran the supply, even with the Waynesboro Works producing fiber at top capacity. Predictably, soon after the launch,

Dupont discovered that – as with rayon and wash-and-wear fabrics – what consumers say they want to the people conducting surveys, and what they actually
want in practice, can be very different. Despite extensive research over many
years that indicated that women did not want to go on wearing heavy girdles,
when lightweight girdles with Lycra finally came on the market, some women
were reluctant to buy them. Having begged for 'a girdle so comfortable that
you don't know you're wearing it', many women found they had no confidence in girdles that didn't grip, and consequently no self-confidence. Girdle
manufacturers – Dupont's direct customers – had to convince store buyers of
their product's efficacy by giving them girdles of Lycra to wear, and suggesting they give out a free tape measure with each girdle of Lycra, so the customer could measure herself in the new girdle and compare it with her
measurements in the old one. Accustomed to the problems of launching
innovative fibers, Dupont redoubled their production of retail marketing
material, supported their customers' advertising and ran various Lycra promotions, and resistance among long-established wearers of the traditional
heavy girdle began to lessen. Within the company, there was a justifiable air
of satisfaction:

> A few years ago, Du Pont textile men began asking a question that one
> wag noted went to the foundation of female fashions: 'What are the
> characteristics of a good girdle?' Not a subject to be decided upon by
> solemn male committee meetings, it was batted up to the consumer her-
> self. And in a series of surveys and test panels, American women replied
> in no uncertain terms. They wanted comfort, coolness, firm support, soft-
> ness, ease of washing, contoured tailoring, fast drying and shape reten-
> tion. From such pronouncements stemmed sizeable events, notably
> continued development of a new product, Lycra spandex fiber, plus the
> starting of a plant to make it. Justification: belief that Lycra can be tai-
> lored to meet these demands and give the consumer what she clearly
> wanted.[24]

But *did* she really want it, and who was '*she*'?

In 1959, as Lycra was being readied for the market, Dupont considered the
demographic projections for the coming 1960s, one of its economists noting:

> The important factor in the 1960s – and one for businessmen to study – is
> the dramatic shift in the age groupings of the population. The most spec-
> tacular increase will be of 18–24 year olds; this group will grow 52 percent
> compared with 2 percent in the 1950s … teenagers will also exert a
> powerful influence.[25]

Yet even before Lycra was launched, there were indications that the women's market that had remained stable for so long was beginning to change. The first signs came in hosiery. Like girdles and other foundations, the wearing of women's stockings had long been considered obligatory and, during World War II, when Dupont's entire nylon fiber output was allocated to military uses, women had gone to extreme lengths to darn and preserve the stockings they had. While sales of nylon stockings had boomed again after the war, ten years on, hosiery manufacturers and retailers, important Dupont customers, began to notice a decline in sales. Following company procedure, in 1956 Dupont commissioned a marketing research study on behalf of the hosiery industry that concluded:

> At the present time, there is clear evidence that the social necessity of wearing hosiery, which was once so powerful, has now lost some of its compelling strength in the face of modern living and the changed social position of women.... There still exists a nucleus of women, both old and young, who are convinced that social necessity is on the side of wearing stockings ... [but] there are many more occasions on average when these young women do not feel the necessity which these elders do ... more younger women than older women find stockings 'uncomfortable', 'inconvenient', '*requiring a girdle*' and 'inappropriate with slacks'.... *It is a truism, applicable to many products, that starting the young person as a consumer of a given product is perhaps the most effective way of perpetuating product use in later years.... This is a danger signal.*[26]

The study identified the years between 12 and 15 as the years when women of all ages felt that young girls should start wearing stockings, and it was in this young age group that resistance was emerging. Through consumption, or rather their rejection of it, the pre-Boomers and oldest female members of the Boomer cohort were beginning to develop an independent profile, but the warning went unheeded. The postwar baby boom had not yet peaked, and elsewhere in the Textile Fibers Division the sales of children's clothes made of Dupont fibers were buoyant. The company continued to assume that the coming generation of little girls would want to be just like their mothers.

By 1960, the year when the first girdles of Lycra went on general sale, the vanguard Boomers were teenagers – the first cohort to be so designated. In 1961, the Christmas gifts Dupont press releases recommended for young teen-agers – blouses with Peter Pan collars and nightdresses with matching lace-trimmed nightcaps that were 'a way of prettily concealing curlers' – were essentially junior versions of what a teenage girl's mother wore. By 1965, such was the steepness of the demographic curve, the teenage market had more than doubled in size, as *Dupont Magazine* reported:

> Teen-Age Boom Rocks the Market. Never before has US business been more preoccupied with the indescribably and ubiquitous phenomenon known as the teen-ager. The nation's population between ages 13 and 19 has mushroomed since WWII to a mighty 24 million, and although they're barely out of childhood, these youngsters are, in the main, sophisticated, informed and discriminating consumers. As such, they're strenuously wooed by businessmen who recognize the awesome power they and their whims can exert in the marketplace.
>
> Last year alone, teenagers spent nearly $15 billion on merchandise. Collectively they accounted for 23 percent of cosmetics sold, nearly half of the motion picture attendance, 40 percent of the record industry's sales, 9 percent of the new cars and an uncounted number of used cars. Today's teen population is increasing at a rate three-times faster than that of the total US population. A New York department store executive notes that today's teenagers represent a whole new social and economic class where *age, not income, is the more precise indicator of consumer demand....* Dupont, a major supplier of the textile fibers utilized by the apparel industry, has not let all this hub-bub go unnoticed. Using features from all media of special interest to teenagers, the knit and woven products groups of Du Pont's Textile Fibers Department this year joined forces in a program to help retailers present new fall teen garments.[27]

Noting that more than 80 percent of teenagers had record collections, and that teenagers had created new dances like the Frug, Watusi and Monkey that they danced in 'popular dance houses called discotheques', Dupont mounted their own travelling rock-and-roll pop concert and musical fashion showcase with fashion editors from *Seventeen* magazine. The showcase went on tour to leading department stores in some thirty major American cities during the August–September back-to-school buying season, promoting teen clothes and accessories made with Dupont fibers and materials. The objective of this pioneering and ambitious campaign, the company said, was 'to create a lasting impression with the teen group who in just a few years will be adult shoppers and *hopefully by then, long standing customers of Dupont'*.[28]

In just four years, Dupont – and the rest of the market in America and Britain – had made the transition from seeing the Boomer generation as a group of dependants, addressed through their parents, to seeing them as a new mass market of consumers to be approached directly and addressed in their own terms. Concentrating on the size of the teenage market, no one in the corporation seems to have considered the possibility that, now that they were making the decisions, Boomers might not want to buy and wear girdles like their mothers

Although the numbers of women in the population arriving at the age of girdle-wearing continued to rise dramatically year by year following Lycra's launch due to the maturing of the baby boom, the sales of girdles of all kinds began to fall. As signposted in Dupont's earlier hosiery study, girls aged 12-to-15 and young women were emerging as the main group of girdle-resisters, and the trend was spreading to other age groups.

No other firm was able to match Dupont's technological expertise, their ability to continually refine and improve fibers in the laboratories, or the company's comprehensive marketing and promotion capabilities: Dupont reacted to falling sales by applying all their resources to the problem. By 1968, Dupont was working on a new kind of foundation especially aimed at the younger market. The technological research behind these new foundations was based on what was described as the first laboratory study of the dynamic forces at work when women wore the garments. Testers were hooked up to specialized monitoring devices including an accelerometer used to measure the rate of 'jiggle in the wiggle', and the effects of the new foundations on body motion, comfort, contour and control were measured. Called 'form-persuasive garments' rather than 'girdles', the new foundations were described as having a 'semi-control' degree of 'hold'. Following Dupont company procedure, the development of these foundations followed market research. In consumer tests of 1,500 women of varying age, weight and dimensions, it was reported that 65 percent had expressed an interest in these new lighter, activity-friendly foundations, with '*interest most pronounced among high school girls and college girls, and older women blessed with trim figures*'.[29] These high school and college girls were the young Boomers, who were arriving in the foundation marketplace in their numbers. Thirty major firms committed to offering their customers new Lycra form persuaders in the coming season, but while Dupont continued to focus on the technical side of fabric innovation, a profound demographic and social shift was taking place. The long-established over-the-counter culture was coming into head-on conflict with the new counterculture.

One day in 1968, the phone rang at Daniel Yankelovich Inc., a small research company in Chicago that specialized in the forecasting of market and social trends. By its own account, this firm had already noted signs of what they called 'the winds of change' among young people, such as a declining interest in white-collar careers, a rising rate of dropping out of school and college, and the emergence of experimental lifestyles, but as yet these changes were vague and unfocused, the values they represented not yet manifest. The telephone call was from the President of Playtex Inc., one of America's largest foundation manufacturers – famous for the '18 Hour Girdle' and 'I Can't Believe It's a Girdle' advertising campaigns – and a major Dupont customer. Concerned and dismayed, he had contacted the company for professional advice. Reporting that his own wife had thrown away her girdle, he asked: 'What does this mean for my business?' (Smith and Clurman 1997: xii). For Playtex, it meant that the company would shift its focus from girdles to brassieres. For the Yankelovich firm, the call constituted a commercial ethnographic moment. In the abandoning of her girdle by the President of Playtex's wife, they saw a materialization of the ways in which Boomers were fundamentally different from previous cohorts in values and attitudes, ultimately leading them to develop a strategy called 'generational marketing', which pioneered the subsequent boom in marketing based on age and cohort characteristics. So what were these characteristics? First – the glorification of youth. Merser (1987) describes the Boomers as the *hope-I-die-before-I-get-old* generation, the cohort 1960s activist Jerry Rubin exhorted: 'Don't grow up. Growing up means giving up your dreams' (Cross 2000). Second, in this revolutionary time of the Civil Rights Movement, the Vietnam War, Women's Lib, the birth-control pill, rock-and-roll, psychedelia, the Watts riots and much more, they wanted nothing to do with the past. Everything had to be new and different – *Burn, baby, burn.*

Bra-burning is always cited as the great symbolic event of the period, but no Boomer woman I spoke to had ever burned a bra, or had personally witnessed one being burned by others. Indeed, brassiere sales continued to rise throughout the 1960s and 1970s in proportion to population growth. But if bra-burning was something of an urban legend, the abandoning of girdles was not, and every Boomer woman I encountered had something to say about it. 'Getting rid of the girdle' emerged as a significant cultural moment, in every sense a defining act of 'emancipation' and 'liberation'. Many of the younger Boomers had refused to wear girdles at all, although many vanguard Boomers had worn them at one time. The following statement is representative of many I obtained from vanguard Boomers; nearly identical to statements made about girdles by women thirty years older, it shows how deeply established the practice had been, and yet how quickly it changed when the social context altered:

> You *had* to wear them, even if you were like me, so skinny that you didn't have anything to hold in. It certainly wasn't sexy. I used to think '*why?*', but you just did it, you *had* to. Your mother made you, for a start. If you didn't, if you just wore regular underwear, people thought it was almost like going out with no underwear on at all. It was *wonderful* when all that stopped.

Some women had consciously thrown their girdles away – 'I dumped them in the garbage' – while others had pushed them to the back of their underwear drawers and just forgotten about them. One Boomer, searching for words to describe abandoning the girdle, said: 'It made me feel free, like that song by the pop group Cream [1966] – "I feel free, I feel free"', and started to sing it. Some vanguard Boomers who were in their late teens and early twenties in the 1960s remembered arguing with their mothers over girdle-wearing, but others – and many of the younger Boomers – recalled that their mothers had eagerly joined them in going girdle-less. It was a major social revolution expressed through stuff that passed largely unnoticed except by the people who made and sold foundations and foundation fibers.

Culture and Commerce: Trying to Save the Girdle

By the mid-1970s, girdle sales in America and Britain were half what they had been in 1965, despite a substantial increase in the female members of the population of girdle-wearing age due to the maturing of the Boomer cohort. As an in-house Dupont report noted with alarm:

> The current market is dominantly older women with no replacement business emerging to take their place. In the 18 to 49 age group that should represent *new* customers that should be with us for years to come, the control garment business has gone down over 50% in just the last six years.[30]

The foundation industry now had to contemplate the possibility that the drop in girdle sales was not just a temporary aberration. Dupont, having wrestled for twenty years with the problems of stress decay, tensile strength, colorfastness and resistance to degradation by gasses, solvents and lights; having undertaken research to establish the existence of a consumer market for lightweight girdles; having developed Lycra for this market and having spent $10,000,000 to produce the perfect elastane fiber for girdles, now found that the market for girdles was fast disappearing for reasons that had nothing to do with the technological capabilities of the product, and everything to do with a change in culture that they and much of America could not understand. Dupont devoted an entire issue of their employee magazine *Better Living* to youth in society, asking – what's it all about?

The magazine revealed a nation divided:

> to the great mass of Americans, the wave of violence and assassination and riots that has engulfed this nation in the 1960s is a distortion of the natural order; to those who have come to maturity in the last decade, it *is* the natural order.[31]

The older generations were perplexed by the fact that the unprecedented affluence enjoyed by the young Boomers had only brought the luxury of dissent. To them, youth's new rites and rituals were incomprehensible: 'New styles of dance suggest Youth's impatience with restraint, belief that emotions are to be trusted. Their music speaks their concern.' The profile of the young Boomer cohort became clearer – and more alarming to producers. Many of the young were dropping out, rejecting corporate life, and the magazine focused on the effect this would have on the business world – where would the employees of tomorrow come from, and how would they be managed? There was as yet little appreciation of the effect youth would have on stuff. The simple demographic projections made when research on Lycra began – that the girdle market would grow as the population grew – had not foreseen the new cultural turn of events. For Dupont, the fiber spinners and weavers, the girdle manufacturers and the retailers of foundations, the question was – could the girdle be saved?

Dupont now commissioned a study by Ernest Dichter Associates, *A Motivational Research Study of the Sales Opportunities for Ladies' Girdles* (1975)[32] which revealed the contesting values and social changes of the age through the medium of a single symbolic mass-produced garment. The problem was clear. To the team's opening question, 'Do you wear a girdle?', the most frequent responses were, 'Thank God, I have not worn one in years' and 'Not yet'. The Dichter team then set out to identify 'old' and 'new' barriers to girdle wearing. Among the former were the perception of girdles as confining and uncomfortable, while the latter reflected the profound shift in lifestyle that had turned the expected certainties of 'The Great Sixties' on their heads. Girdles, the team reported, were not 'in' and they went against 'women's lib ideas'. Women perceived girdles as an instrument of male chauvinism – a typical reply was, 'What would men say if we asked them to wear girdles?' Girdles had been associated with the 'dressed-up' look, but now women were 'revolting against fashion dictates', and girdles didn't go together with the new widespread desire for informality, it was the 'let-it-all-hang-out' era. The 'return to naturalness' was a strong recurrent theme. The new emphasis was on 'being real', 'being yourself', 'doing your own thing', 'doing what you feel', and girdles were seen as being antithetical to the new morality in which the authentic was valued and the fake rejected. It was considered 'immoral to try to mislead or deceive'. Girdles were seen as doing just that, and if women wore them, it would be embarrassing to be found out. Increased activity was also becoming a factor – 'Today girls exercise. We used to let a girdle do the work for us.' Unusually, the Dichter team polled men as well as women on the subject, duly reporting that 'men are turned off by girdles'. To men, girdles 'were an automatic stop sign', 'like a brick wall', uncool. As one man put it, using phrases that young Boomers found damning, 'A chick with a girdle isn't free … she's just not with it.'

The team had been provided with sketches of new 'concept girdles', which could be developed if there was a positive response. One was a 'Do-It-Yourself' girdle with detachable parts, which a woman could customize at home depending on her figure needs. Another was the 'Jeangirdle'. Informal denim jeans were seen by foundation makers as the enemy of the formal clothing that depended on girdle-wearing to look good. The 'Jeangirdle' aimed to subvert the trend by sewing girdles into jeans: apart from flattening the tummy and slimming the thighs, the inbuilt girdle was supposed to improve the look of a woman's bottom. There was guarded interest, but concern was expressed that the girdle should not be visible. Jeans were the emblematic garment of authenticity, so they would not want to be 'found out'. The Dichter report concluded that women did not want to go back to the old girdles, and a 'New Girdle 1975' had to be created that was 'progressive, looking ahead, an advance in fashion and psychology'. Above all else, it must not be called a girdle.

The company then commissioned a two-part marketing research study on control undergarments from Brand, Gruber and Company, primarily for the benefit of the foundation industry and retailers of foundations. The first part was reassuring in tone, largely telling the industry what it wanted to hear – that 'figure control garments could once again be the profit center they were in the past', denied that 'in this age of "letting it all hang out" women no longer wanted figure control', and suggested that poor sales were due primarily to 'antiquated merchandising'.[33] To remedy this, the report focused on sales techniques that emphasized the needs of the clothes, rather than the customer's bodily imperfections. 'The non-girdle wearer' it reported would 'refuse to buy "figure therapy"'. She would 'buy the undergarment only because the pantsuit needs it, not because her body needs it'.[34] The theory was that every garment could be presented as having a 'need' – trousers needed the 'panty ridge' to be eliminated, high-waisted slacks needed midriff holding and so on. If women had objections to being controlled, they hopefully would not object to being in control of their clothes, using new lightweight girdles designed for particular items of clothing. The second Brand Gruber study focused on women aged 35 and younger – mainly Boomers – and on one kind of girdle in particular, the long line all-in-one – which had been identified as a garment that might particularly appeal to non-girdle wearers. Sessions took place in rooms where the walls were hung with foundation garments, and women were asked which ones they preferred – not whether they wanted to wear foundations in the first place. Nonetheless, the attitudes that emerged during the sessions were unanimously and resoundingly negative, virtually identical to the account given to me by Boomers twenty-five years later.

As the report noted:

> There was a consistent recounting of tales of 'giving up the girdle'. The
> normal undergarment pattern among these women included bra and
> panty hose. With the exception of the very youngest women, almost
> everyone had, at one time or another, been a regular girdle wearer. Girls
> frequently went into girdles at their mother's insistence and continued to
> wear them 'as if there was a law stating that they must'. A number of
> women were told by their mother that 'nice girls' always wear girdles and
> that 'fanny jiggle' was in poor taste. Most of the sample had given up
> girdle wearing some years ago. A number of women, however, have kept
> one or two girdles for use with special outerwear which requires a
> 'smooth' look. We found literally no woman who enjoyed or felt comfort-
> able wearing a girdle. They appeared quite delighted that society no
> longer demanded the wearing of a girdle, and indicated antipathy toward
> the idea that girdles might one day again become de rigueur ... new fash-
> ions or not, they would be damned if they would give up the 'new under-
> garment lifestyle' to which they had only recently and happily entered.[35]

The focus then shifted to the retail sector. Leading retailers were invited by
the market-research firm to 'wide-open-give-and-take' forums and presented
with the key research findings to date: that women were happy to have shed
girdles, that they disliked girdles, that 'women used to believe that there was a
"law" that they had to wear girdles' and most believe the law has been
repealed. Also, that the higher the socioeconomic class and the younger the
women, the more negative the attitude to the girdle – 'the lower the socioeconomic class and the older the woman, the more like old times'. The retailers were then asked: *what has happened to the girdle market? Is it dying?* At first,
the responses were guarded – 'It appears there was initial reticence to admit
the "facts" to an "outsider"' – but probing revealed that, while the sales of bras
had increased, there had been substantial losses in girdle sales, and by the end
of the sessions, retailers were even vying with each other to tell stories about
how bad things were. Presented with a possible savior in the form of the new
all-in-one, the retailers did not respond as the investigators had hoped. While
the manufacturers and market researchers had been struggling to get people
to differentiate between different kinds of girdles, the investigators found that,
to many of the people present, 'A girdle is a girdle no matter if it's a heavy,
control paneled garment, a wispy sensual all-in-one or a Lycra-added panty.
They understood all classes to be girdles.'[36] The report concluded with a
description of a decimated girdle market serviced by demoralized girdle retailers who felt there was little they could do to remedy the situation. Taken

together, these accounts provide unique insights into the power of implicit cultural rules and ideologies, and the way their overthrow manifested on the level of everyday life.

So what was going on? From the perspective of the present, the 1960s can be seen as a time of deep contradictions and sweeping social change in the United States. The economy was strong, but even as unprecedented levels of personal income in some sectors, and new heights of mass production and mass consumption were reached, cracks began to appear in the facade of the Great Society. Social inequalities of race and gender became ever-more apparent, inspiring both non-violent political idealism and violent political action. The pre-Boomers and vanguard members of the Boomer cohort, who had grown up in conditions of unprecedented economic growth and affluence, began to reject the values of capitalism and the materialistic American way of life. Influential new socio-political movements emerged, notably civil rights, women's liberation and what became known as the sexual revolution, as seen in more detail in Chapter 5. In the 1970s, economic recession and rising unemployment contributed to the strains of social change, and completed the dismantling of strong social control that had begun in the previous decade. As the defining garment of social and patriarchal control, the girdle had to go. Its abandonment was political action on the personal level, an act of liberation through stuff.

It is clear how both the political/economic and the feminist approaches to the girdle fit in to the social and historical context outlined above, but it is useful here to consider a cultural and anthropological paradigm that gives a perspective that is different to either. Known as 'Cultural Theory' it is particularly relevant to the events described here and in Chapter 5, as well as to anthropology at home in general. 'Cultural Theory' was originated by Mary Douglas as an anthropological approach to studying complex institutions, social organization, ways of thought and behavior. It aims to free analyses from historical, political, ideological and political specificities, or rather to situate them in a more holistic, dynamic framework, the better to reveal cultural values and processes at work. At the heart of Cultural Theory is Douglas' concept of 'grid and group', a way of categorizing and analyzing societies and organizations according to whether or not they are 'high grid' or 'low grid', 'high group' or 'low group'. As summarized by Rayner (1992), a 'high group' way of life is characterized by a high degree of social control and a 'low group' the reverse; 'high grid' is characterized by conspicuous hierarchical forms of social stratification and strong authority structures, while 'low grid' is associated with egalitarian forms and relations. Different combinations result in different social and cultural dynamics, ways of thinking and patterns of behavior. Once you know what the grid and group configuration of a particular organization or society is, you can better understand why it works the way it does, and predict how it is likely to react under conditions of change. Cultural Theory has been elaborated and applied to fields that include risk analysis, environmental studies, the study of business and management, household studies and information science, and detailed definitions and descriptions of 'grid' and 'group' by Douglas can be found in several of her key works, including *Natural Symbols* (1996) and *Cultural Bias* (1978), and see *Cultural Theory* (Thompson *et al.* 1990). For our purposes, the basic concept of a four-square typology, with each of the four types characterized by different values, organizational forms and material culture is sufficient to move us toward an anthropological understanding of cultural dynamics under capitalism, as seen here through Lycra.

To use Douglas' terminology, the pre-World War II and 1950s society in which girdle-wearing was obligatory was a society of high grid and high group in the grip of a complex regulative cosmos (Douglas 1996: 141), which the girdle embodied and symbolized. In such societies, any small deviation is anathema, ritual is well-established and alternative views of how life could be different are totally absent. Yet societies also change, and in time the very strength and rigidity of strong grid and group lead to resistance and rejection among the rank and file members of society, who come to feel that the 'persons in control behave to them mechanically and treat them as if they were objects' (Douglas 1996: 153), instilling in them the desire to wrest

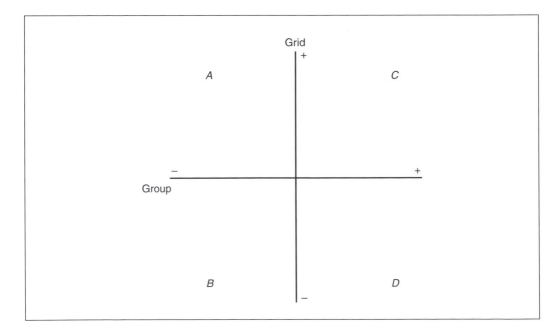

Figure 4.4 Mary Douglas, four-square grid and group box. Courtesy of Routledge.

control and exert it themselves. As noted by Douglas, uniform and controlling dress is characteristic of strong grid and group society. Again – the girdle had to go.

However, despite the damning evidence of their market research, Dupont was not prepared to abandon a market in which so much had been invested, or customers with whom they had worked for so long. Following procedure, Dupont submitted the problem of falling girdle sales to in-house problem-solving processes. Brainstorming had been replaced by Synectics, another form of creative idea-generation meeting. By now, the very word 'girdle' had become unattractive, even to the producers. In future, if at all possible, it would not be used. Instead, the terms 'innerwear', 'intimate apparel' and 'bodywear' were introduced. Dupont attendees were asked to focus on how and where, in an ideal world, the new all-in-ones and other foundation garments could be presented to the public. As with brainstorming, participants were encouraged to be as audacious as possible in their suggestions, which included:[37]

- see-through all-in-ones on the cover of *Playboy* and *Penthouse* magazines;
- the first front-cover presentation of underwear on *Vogue* magazine;
- the leading lady tennis star of the day posing in a white all-in-one and tiny tennis skirt in *Sports Illustrated* magazine;
- a leading feminist modeling a leopard print all-in-one in *MS* magazine;
- the female vocalist of a San Francisco psychedelic rock band, modeling a gold all-in-one in *Rolling Stone* magazine.

This was a fantasy wish list, which never went further than internal circulation at Dupont, but it shows what an important part of popular culture magazines had become, how aware some people at Dupont were of the new cultural trends and how they would have liked to subvert the counterculture if it were possible. It wasn't, in 1975.

Dupont continued to promote girdles and all-in-ones, sending out press releases that sought to overcome resistance by using catchphrases of the time: 'Remember when the young were saying "let it all hang out"? That expression has been replaced by "get it all together".'[38] And 'Women's Bodygarments Have Been Liberated Too',[39] as well as 'Put On The Power'.[40]

One advertisement for a Lycra brassiere and girdle, the latter tactfully halfway out of the picture, attempted to use the language of the Women's Movement: 'Lycra, the mark of a real woman ... Makes *your* mark in this man's world.'

The positive aspects of the market-research surveys were edited and used to compile booklets entitled, *The Hidden Market Potential In 'Control' Garments*[41] and *Control Garments: Do They Have a Future? Three Major New Du Pont Consumer Studies Say Yes! If ...*[42] which Dupont circulated to their customers to 'help rebuild, recapture and revamp your undergarment business'.[43]

One national promotional campaign was themed 'Today's Look Calls for Lycra': foundations in Lycra were displayed next to the clothes they were supposed to be worn under; and, as a central feature of store displays, there was a special telephone customers could pick up 'for a one-minute information-packed message on bras and foundations made with Lycra'.[44] In the wake of the marketing-research surveys, the company conducted Idea Generation Meetings[45] in which they sought to create positive new 'positions' or associations, images and meanings for Lycra undergarments. 'Hug and Cling', 'Sleek Line' and 'Natural Enhancement' were among the suggestions, but in the climate of the times, none of them took root. Undeterred, the company conducted national campaigns to promote the new all-in-one 'Clothes Smoothers with Lycra' and manufacturers went on producing 'under-dressing

Figure 4.5 Lycra: the Mark of a Real Woman, courtesy of Hagley Museum and Library.

The Lycra® money-makers!

More and more manufacturers are making them.

More and more retailers are promoting them.

And more and more women are looking smoother, sleeker, more natural in their clothes.

Convince a woman that Clothes Smoothers will make her outerwear look better—and you've got the key to selling her. And making new customers.

That's one of the major findings in the three consumer-research studies in the Du Pont report. To sell Clothes Smoothers as a solution to woman's clothes problems—not her body problems.

And the variety of these light-weights is growing because Lycra®

spandex has the broadest denier and product types. The result is the widest fabric versatility in the trade.

With manufacturers and retailers coming up with new ideas, new designs, new reasons for customers to buy—they'll buy.

This is what started it all.

Du Pont research initiated the major change in philosophy which turned yesterday's "undergarments" into today's Clothes Smoothers.

*Du Pont registered trademark.

Figure 4.6 The Lycra Money-Makers!, courtesy of Hagley Museum and Library.

Today's Look Calls for Lycra® SPANDEX by Manufacturer

Fashion is all different now, and foundations of "Lycra"* spandex have helped to shape this welcome revolution. New clothes should be free and easy, bright, sophisticated in a fun manner, barer than ever if you like. Most especially, everything must be easy to move in.

Breathe a sigh of relief. Gone, with the corseted look, are the girdles that imprisoned the body, jabbed and poked. What goes on before the new kind of clothes: foundations of "Lycra". Never before has such great control been so gentle. Fabrics of "Lycra" are softer. You get a sleek, smooth line that looks like it's all slim, svelte you. You'll like the way they wash, they wear. Do visit our foundation department soon and ask, "What's new—in 'Lycra'?"

*Du Pont registered trademark

STORE NAME

Figure 4.7 Today's Look Calls for Lycra, courtesy of Hagley Museum and Library.

garments' with evocative names like 'Free Spirit', but for all Dupont's efforts and those of the manufacturers, the obligatory wearing of the girdle did not revive. Even Barbie dolls no longer wore them. As far as the mass market was concerned, the girdle was dead.

5

LYCRA, AEROBICS AND THE RISE OF THE LEGGING

The ethnographic moment in which a Boomer woman couldn't find Lycra workout leggings to buy had its roots in another time, and in places like this, a vanguard aerobics studio in Beverly Hills, Los Angeles, where I carried out fieldwork in 1979, and witnessed the rebirth of Lycra.

They filed through the narrow doorway, trailing fresh cool air into the humid atmosphere of the room, neatly sidestepping the patches of sweat on the floor from the previous class. Dance bags were flung against the back and side walls, and they spread themselves out into staggered rows. Some, darting quickly and confidently, moved into position to form the first two rows facing the mirrored front walls, standing with legs akimbo to stake their territory. Others made up rows behind them, spacing themselves so as to be able to see as much of their reflections as possible through the spaces left by those at the front. The less confident stood at the rear, hugging the back wall, standing directly behind those in front of them so as not to be seen. No one paid any attention to the short Hispanic cleaning lady who scuttled up and down the rows, stabbing ineffectually at the damp patches on the wooden floor with a large mop.

A tall girl, hair pulled back in a pony tail, forehead encircled in a toweling sweatband, bounced into the room. She wore shiny Lycra leggings under trim red shorts, a tank top leotard, legwarmers and the new white Reebok Freestyle aerobics shoes. Everyone else was dressed in a similar way, minus the shorts which served as a kind of staff uniform. Some of the class members wore sweatshirts which they would remove when they got hot and tie around their waists. Others sported short t-shirts that had been cropped from longer ones, or sweat-pants made of what looked like plastic rubbish bin liners, which were supposed to keep your muscles warm and make you sweat more when you exercised. These were serious clothes, dancer's clothes, dark in color so as not to show the sweat. Suddenly there was a flurry of activity, as some late-comers entered and made their way toward the rear, looking like parrots amidst a flock of crows. Dressed in toning leotards, leggings, legwarmers and sweatbands in bright yellow, pink, turquoise and emerald green, they were in full makeup with elaborately styled hair, and all were wearing lots of heavy jewelry that was obviously real. They did not look like they intended to sweat. 'Persians' someone hissed at me by way of explanation. In the wake of the fall of the Shah of Iran, Los Angeles had recently experienced an influx of moneyed Persians who were attempting to integrate themselves into what were considered to be fashionable activities by the locals.

Ready? The teacher's voice flattened the murmuring in the room.

Those in the front rows tossed their heads and bridled like runners about to mount the starting blocks, shaking their arms and legs to loosen them. A few had dropped into a crouch and were doing warm-up squats and lunges.

Anyone new today?

There was a hesitant flutter of hands in the very back row.

Right. Slow down if you get tired, be careful, but remember you won't get anywhere unless you push yourself. So now – let's work out!

Loud disco music flooded the room and the teacher took up her position at the front, facing the first row, moving and calling out in time with the beat.

Eight front sides and back. Down through four and two, let's go!

Knowing the routine, the 'regulars' in the front rows plunged into a series of rhythmic bends and kicks, moving with the precision of a chorus line, eyes switching between the teacher and their own reflections in the mirror. The middle rows followed, half a beat behind. Those at the very back, still struggling to understand what was expected of them, went into action with varying degrees of success, falling well behind the middle rows in timing, in the manner of a Mexican wave. The Persians did very little. They behaved as though they thought it sufficient simply to be present.

Now push! We need to WORK!

The music shifted into higher gear, propelling them through stretches, crouches, squats, lunges and lifts, making them breathe more and more deeply, pushing up the temperature of the room with each exhalation. The beat changed and the front row shifted easily into a series of high kicks alternating with intense bursts of running in place, arms punching the air over their heads. Faces flushed, foreheads running with sweat, they swung into a series of spinning star jumps. The back row, panting, had reached the end of their endurance. The middle rows were faltering, concentration and stamina draining away, but those at the front continued to move as one, exuberant yet controlled, eyes fixed on the mirror. The music pulsed up and the teacher's voice rang out,

This is YOUR workout. You should ENJOY it. Now SMILE!

In his 1986 study of health, fitness, sport and American society 1830–1940, Green noted a correspondence between social change and the kind of sports that become popular, while Hardy (1990) suggested the attractive term '*sportgeist*' to describe the way in which physical practice accommodates and reflects the social values of a particular time and place. Stuff, as we have seen, also embodies values and ideology. For the women of the Boomer cohort, in the crucible of social and cultural change that gave rise to the early aerobic movement, Lycra captured, constructed and clothed the *sportgeist*.

Aerobics as Ecstatic Religion

Given the fame they would later achieve through fitness books, video, films and television shows, the early aerobics studios were strikingly basic and a far cry from the polished, elaborate commercial spa-gyms of the 1980s and 1990s.

There were no annual membership fees, no waiting lists. You simply turned up to 'take a class', paying about $5 a time in Los Angeles and New York and £1 in London, another early center of the movement that centered on Debbie Moore's Pineapple Dance Studios in Covent Garden. The procedure was similar to that long followed by professional dancers, who have to exercise regularly in order to keep supple. Dancers were accustomed to moving around town and between towns, looking for classes to take and rooms to rehearse in, and to following their teachers, guru-like, from studio to studio. The difference in the new aerobics routines was that rhythmic callisthenic movements had been substituted for the classical ballet steps and rock music for conventional ballet and adagio music, making the classes more accessible and attractive to non-professionals. As in ballet studios, there was no equipment. No stationary bicycles, treadmills, rowing machines, cross trainers or other gym paraphernalia, just an empty room – and bodies, lots of Boomer bodies.

What was striking at the time was the transcendent nature of the movement of which the aerobics classes were just one part. It was a total social phenomenon that spread into dietary practices; beliefs about health and medicine, new music and other forms of popular culture, new codes of dress and behavior, new attitudes to the body. It pervaded every aspect of everyday life, and was pursued so widely and with such enthusiasm that the word 'craze' was applied from the beginning. So what was going on?

Fitness and exercise initially received relatively little critical academic attention, reflecting the privileging of the theorized body over the observed and lived body, and the preference during much of the 1980s for studies of organized team and spectator sports. More recently, a predominantly sociological literature on individual fitness has arisen, summarized in Maguire's excellent *Fit for Consumption*, which locates exercise as a highly significant cultural field at the intersection of larger social processes, an arena in which 'individuals and institutions, producers and consumers, struggle over the status and definitions of fitness and fit bodies' (Maguire 2007: 8). These recent studies deal with the mass commercialization of contemporary fitness, focusing on key sites and issues such as health clubs, fitness media, fitness services provided by fitness trainers, the problems of hegemonic body image and the place of 'fitness' in the current public discourse of personal responsibility for health. These are important considerations in the present, but they do not explain the extraordinary popularity of the early aerobics movement, before it became the institutionalized and commercialized practice it is today, or the relationship of aerobics to the fundamental social and cultural changes of the 1960s and 1970s in which Lycra, Dupont and the women of the Boomer cohort became entangled.

The received opinion among attendees of the early aerobics classes – often explicitly stated in the first examples of what would later become an avalanche of fitness books, videos and magazines but was passed by word of mouth initially – was that regular aerobic exercise was a panacea of the first order. As I observed both at the time and from the perspective of the present, three levels of meaning were conflated in this received wisdom about aerobics that was part of the popular culture of the time – the physiological (the inner workings of the aerobics process), the physical (the surface appearance or image) and the metaphysical (the discourse of spiritual improvement and betterment) – a trinity that within anthropology suggests that aerobics was not just an exercise class but the manifestation of new values and ideologies in which Lycra would play a key role.

This takes us back to Chapter 4, and Douglas's grid and group theory in which the disappearance of the girdle was seen as arising from the breakdown of the strong grid/strong group society of the 1950s and early 1960s. When change comes, there is a short transitional period that Douglas identified as a 'millennial' moment and Durkheim called a period of 'effervescence', characterized by what Douglas calls the 'millennial' posture:

> The millennialist … believes in a Utopian world in which goodness of heart can prevail without institutional devices. He does not seek to cherish any particular social forms. He would sweep them all away. The millennialist goes in for frenzies; he welcomes the letting-go experience.… He seeks bodily ecstasy which, by expressing for him the explosive advent of a new age, reaffirms the value of the doctrine.
>
> (Douglas 1996: xxxvi–xxxvii)

From the perspective of the present, this passage well describes many of the aspects of the 1960s and 1970s, with aerobics emerging as a public form of bodily ecstasy linking many elements of the new ideologies and values. This moves us from the sociology of sport to the anthropological paradigm of physical activity as symbolic bodily practice. Coming rather late to the field, anthropology is now making important contributions to the understanding of sport and physical activity in contemporary Western society, particularly those non-team practices such as the martial arts (Donohue 1993), surfing (Lanagan 2002), extreme sports (Palmer 2002), running (Mewett 2002) and triathlon (Granskog 1993) that have risen to prominence since the 1960s and are widely seen by practitioners and observers as involving 'something more' than mere physical exertion (Donohue 1993: 105).

Essentially works of symbolic anthropology, influenced by Mary Douglas, Clifford Geertz and Victor Turner, these studies see key physical activities primarily as rituals and rites of passage, generating intense experiences that allow participants to reach 'epiphanic' or sudden deep insights into the essence or meaning of things while also providing a means of giving these insights physical expression. These insights can be personal or sociocultural. As Blanchard (1995: 53), following Douglas, put it, because sport always reflects the basic values of the cultural setting within which it is actually performed, it functions as a ritual 'transmitter of culture'. Within anthropology it has long been recognized that ritual dance, like sport, is a means through which altered states of consciousness are attained. As Lewis (1989) pointed out, in ecstatic religion there is a complex relationship at play between chemical catalysts (endorphins) and sociocultural dynamics. When stimulated by intense physical activity such as dancing, the body's endorphin system contributes to the ecstatic experience – as does the 'heightened ritually marked sociality' (Comaroff and Comaroff 1992: 78) that moving in unison produces. Ecstatic dance expresses ideologies and values on a communal level, while creating community and solidarity among the dancers. The early aerobic movement can be seen as a highly significant symbolic body practice, a form of ecstatic religion in which many elements came together and were given expression during a 'millennial shift'.

What were these elements? Key among them were the rise of youth- and pop culture, the Women's Movement and the so-called 'Diet Revolution'; all bespeak the desire to wrest control that characterizes millennial shifts.

The millennial moment of the 1960s had a unique demographic dimension that gave rise to 'youth culture' as the vanguard Boomers began to come of age. As the largest cohort in history, their very numbers gave them a resonance, power, homogeneity and identity they might otherwise have lacked. This is not to say that all young people actively participated in the counterculture of the 1960s, that all who did participate were young, or that 'revolution' and 'change' had consistent, monolithic meanings. Initially, the impetus for change grew up around groups such as students, sites such as universities and urban centers, artifacts such as popular music and culture, and issues such as civil rights, gender equality and peace, diffusing from these sites through the 1960s and 1970s. Other manifestations, mainly associated with youth initially, were sexual freedom and the rise of what became known as the mind, body and spirit movement, the latter signifying a rejection of established Western spiritual beliefs and conventional therapies. New ways of dressing developed that constituted a visible rejection of 1950s values – the wearing of working-class clothes (jeans and work shirts) by middle-class youth alluded to by Sahlins in Chapter 1; the popularity of fantasy psychedelic shirts, 'Renaissance' costumes or long 'country' dresses worn in town that challenged the conventions of time and place; hair worn long and 'natural' by both sexes instead of in the short, controlled styles that had been favored; young men assuming colorful and highly individualistic clothing where once they had been expected to dress soberly and uniformly in gray flannel suits. Fitting the millennial paradigm, youth wanted to be in control themselves, and among young women of the cohort, as seen in Chapter 4, a defining act of rejecting social constraints was the abandoning of the girdle.

The anti-materialism that characterized the young Boomers as part of their rejection of Establishment values would later contribute to their embracing of exercise during the millennial shift. The importance of 'fitness' was brought home to many young American Boomers in 1957, when Russia beat America into space with the launch of Sputnik, an event that set off a searching official inquiry into the state of the American nation. It focused, among other things, on the ability of school-age children – the young Boomers – to meet what was seen as a Soviet challenge of crisis proportions. Over forty years later, Boomer women remembered the national education tests and physical fitness assessments carried out at the time in every school in the country, in a general atmosphere of alarm and anxiety. Boomers, the eldest of whom were then aged twelve, were the first cohort for which television, convenience foods and family car ownership were the norm. Tests revealed that they were less fit than their parents' generation had been and, it was assumed, less fit and educationally able than Russian children were. The test results drove reforms that saw more teaching of math and science in schools, and a national program of physical education promotion that continued through the 1960s, and was aimed at adults as well as at children, reaching into schools, homes and workplaces. For many, the paradox of plenty (see Lears 1994; Potter 1954) was being brought home: what had previously been perceived to be 'progress' and the good life was now beginning to be seen as the cause of a softening of physical, mental and moral fiber. It was a theme that would re-surface in later years.

The emergent Women's Movement also fit the millennial model. As with 'youth', the movement had diverse elements, but for all, gaining control – wresting it from patriarchal authority, enabling women to take control of their own lives, health, bodies, sexuality and reproduction – was paramount. There is an extensive literature on the movement that can be consulted for further background, Here, in the specific context of the millennial shift and aerobics, I cite one of the most influential and explicit statements of the thinking of the times among politicized women. It comes from the hugely influential book on women's health – *Our Bodies, Our Selves* – cited by Nader (1997: 717) as a landmark work that sought to crack controlling paradigms by 'introducing women to their own bodies as a site for the exercise of power':

For us, body education is core education. Our bodies are the physical bases from which we move out into the world; ignorance, uncertainty –

even, at worst, shame – about our physical selves create in us an aliena-
tion from ourselves that keeps us from being the whole people we could
be. Picture a woman trying to do work and to enter into equal and satisfy-
ing relationships with other people when she feels physically weak
because she has never tried to be strong; when she drains her energy
trying to change her face, her figure, her hair, her smells to match some
ideal norm set by magazines and TV.

(Boston Women's Health Collective 1973: iii)

This statement, which contextualizes the giving up of the girdle, resonated
strongly with the nascent aerobics movement, which would provide women
with an entirely new way of transforming themselves, on their own terms. Of
all forms of exercise, aerobics was then – and remains – practiced almost
entirely by women.

At the same time as the formation of youth culture and the transformation
of women's rights and health, another element of the millennial shift emerged
– what came to be called the 'Diet Revolution'. Again, this was not a monolithic movement, but it drew many strands and influences together, transmut-
ing changing social values into new dietary practices. A seminal work of the
movement was a cookbook, *Laurel's Kitchen*. Written in Berkeley, California, in
the mid-1960s, it presented a revolutionary portrait of a holistic vegetarian lifestyle that fundamentally challenged existing red-meat-and-potatoes mainstream practice. As much a work of spiritual guidance as of culinary practice, it
begins with a narrative in which a newcomer encounters this new way of life
for the first time:

Tubs of beans, all colors and shapes, surrounded me, and barrels of
noodles – buckwheat, whole wheat, soy and spinach. Everything was
beautiful: earthen-colored and completely free of cellophane wrappers.
Moving about me confidently on every side were lithe, tawny young men
and women in faded blue denims, peasant blouses and skirts made from
old bedspreads, their thick manes braided, rubber-banded or falling free.
I was painfully aware of my wash-and-wear shirtwaist dress.

(Robertson *et al.* 1976: 39; my italics)

In the 1940s and 1950s, the buzzword had been 'convenience', and innovations were meant to make life easier and to save time, or presented by advertisers as though they did – 'standard American' (North-Western European)
cuisine boasted casseroles made with tinned or dehydrated soup, the first Betty
Crocker cake mixes and the first pre-packaged 'TV' dinners that only needed
reheating in the oven. Now, in the 1960s millennial shift, this was reversed.

Time spent in cooking was not now seen as time lost, but as 'meaning' gained, and instead of 'making easy' there was a new discourse of 'making hard' – chopping, stirring, kneading and peeling 'real' food. In this new system of values, nothing of true worth was believed to come easily or quickly, and the meaning of 'the good life' was transformed. Parallel to the 'natural' food movement was the rejection of synthetic fibers – the 'revolt against polyester' – and the return to popularity of natural fibers, as described by Schneider (1994).

Aerobics was the symbolic bodily practice that tied these and other elements of the millennial shift together through ecstatic practice. A key text for the period, in which the ideology of aerobics and the fitness movement generally is made explicit, is *Jane Fonda's Workout Book*. Published in 1981 but reflecting the influences and beliefs that had been emerging since the 1960s, it resonates with *Our Bodies, Our Selves* and *Laurel's Kitchen*. Like them, it is a book of both physical and metaphysical practice, in which the narrative and transformative elements are strong. It begins with the story of Fonda's own progress from the 1960s Hollywood starlet of stereotyped appearance who strove to embody the cultural ideal in which a woman could never be too blonde or too thin, through a period of political activism in the early 1970s in which she gained insight into forms of social control from which she was now alienated – 'the women of Vietnam had become victims of the same *Playboy* culture that had played havoc with me' (Fonda 1981: 20) – finally arriving at the realization that, after working out, women 'felt better about themselves, held their heads higher and looked more comfortable in their bodies' (Fonda 1981: 23). The book included detailed instructions for exercise, recipes for healthy eating and general guidelines on women's health, offering women a way of 'breaking the weaker sex mold', of making a positive commitment to change.

Striking a deep chord in the popular psyche of women across the United States and in many places abroad, it was an instant bestseller. In the phraseology of the time, aerobic exercise was perceived by vanguard adherents as empowerment, the wresting back of control of one's own body, life and health. If weight loss and change in body shape transpired as a result of exercise, these were by-products of a more meaningful activity, not an end in itself. The very practice of highly energetic exercise by women – smelly, sweaty, strenuous activity – challenged the old construct of the 'ideal' controlled and passive woman. Far more important than appearance was the empowerment – physical, psychological, social – that was perceived to come through exercise. These emergent, young, liberated, millennial females, mainly of the Boomer cohort, constituted a new social category in Sahlins' terms, and aerobics was a new physical and symbolic practice that defined them. But what new clothes

Figure 5.1 Jane Fonda's New Workout video, image courtesy of the Advertising Archives.

would construct and consolidate the new category? Women looking to the *Jane Fonda Workout Book* for guidance, found this:

> Dress for it. An exercise outfit helps because it sets this time apart from the rest of the day and makes it matter more. I prefer a leotard and tights.... I always wear leg warmers to keep my leg muscles warm – and

because they make me feel like a dancer. You should feel comfortable and able to move freely.

(Fonda 1981: 70)

And this is when Lycra made its reappearance.

Lycra and Aerobics

Like the class/studio set up, aerobic exercise clothes grew out of dance, in which the basic all-in-one leotard or combinations of a leotard top and long footless tights, all in knitted jersey fabrics, usually black, had long been standard. Ease of movement, shape retention, durability, moisture-management and warmth are the prime considerations in dance, and dancers had always customized and accessorized their dance wear. In the 1970s, a new Dupont invention originally intended for use in lingerie – shiny Antron nylon mixed with Lycra – had proved to be vastly superior to the fabrics previously in use for dance wear. The new Lycra–Antron blend made possible new cut-and-sew techniques that resulted in garments that hugged the body and moved with it in a way that had never been possible before. Established ballet dancewear manufacturers took it up enthusiastically, using it for traditional leotards and leggings in the classic black or pale pink, but the real changes emerged from another quarter.

The death of the girdle, the decline in traditional lingerie and the resultant slump in the foundation market generally had resulted in a surplus of Dupont Antron–Lycra fabrics in a range of fashion colors originally intended for undergarments, which now reposed unused in warehouses. Small craft businesses grew up, centered first around dance seamstresses who bought the unwanted shiny stretch fabric and used it to make colorful dancewear for private clients. As one Boomer remembered:

One of the women who worked in the gym did it as a sideline. Lots of people were doing it then. You could have whatever you wanted. She had samples of the colors and styles, and you could put together the most amazing combinations. The colors were so bright, so intense. Real look-at-me stuff. Yellows, purples, anything. It didn't look at all out of place at the time. And the great thing was you could have something that no one else had. I had some leggings that were different colors on each leg. And then there were all the other bits, the legwarmers, those little stretch belts, the headbands, the wristbands. What was so wonderful was that it was completely new. We'd never had anything like it before.

Another woman recalled:

> In 1975, I spent some time in Los Angeles. The whole fitness thing was just beginning, and I had an aunt who was a real shopper. Always Rodeo Drive. In the sales, but still Rodeo Drive. She was always into the latest things, whatever was hot, and she was into yoga. She got me my first leotard to wear to yoga classes, from a special kind of shop. It was wonderful, I'd never seen anything like it. Navy blue, with cap sleeves and flashes of color up around the shoulder. And there was another one, a kind of crossover style in this shiny material that turned out to be Lycra. It felt just great wearing them, they didn't feel like anything I'd ever worn before, so sort of free. We ended up going to yoga, an hour and a half, every single day. That was the way things were. There was a feeling you had to keep at it, all the time. And then there were the leggings, you had to have the leggings. There was a guy in the class who wore them, he also had a pony tail, and people used to give him some very odd looks.

In one of the many ironies that surround Lycra, what had been the ultimate fiber of control now became the defining fiber of freedom. In the past, women had worn girdles beneath their garments to make the clothes look good. In other words, women were worn by their clothes. Now Lycra, the aerobics movement and the wider culture turned this paradigm on its head. Lycra leggings and leotards allowed women to wear their own bodies. Lycra became the second skin for a new life in which self-confidence would be rooted in women and their bodies, not in rules, dress codes, wearing clothes that were 'appropriate' for age or social status, and especially not in wearing girdles. It facilitated the emergence of empowered bodies that owed nothing to patriarchal notions of propriety or the erotic. This was a moral body, a body that was perceived as 'good' because it was 'real' and 'natural', although both categories are culturally determined (Douglas 1996: 73). Now women were going to do their own thing.

The values in contention during the period of transformation can be summarized in the following oppositions:

Control by others/Control by self
Mainstream medicalization/Alternative therapy
Convenience food/'Real' food
'Making easy' (ease valued)/'Making hard' (effort valued)
Synthetic fibers and fabrics/Natural fibers and fabrics
Passive/Active
Lycra girdle/Lycra leggings

Lycra so perfectly embodied and facilitated the expression of the new cultural values and ideologies that it was able to counter the trend and cross over from one oppositional pole to the other, becoming the 'synthetic' through which the 'natural' was made manifest. In the midst of the rejection of convention and convenience epitomized by the 'wash and wear shirtwaister dress', Lycra was the exception – the one synthetic fiber that not only countered the trend but became iconic. Wearing the new Lycra exercise clothes was not just a fashion statement: it was a social statement in material form. And in a striking example of cultural blindness, few in the mainstream seemed to realize that the beloved 'new' stretch fiber was the very stuff of which the hated and rejected girdle had been made.[1] Or that leotards and leggings looked identical to the new all-in-one foundation garments.

New exercisers found the experience of wearing leotards and leggings of Lycra exhilarating, liberating and revolutionary. Lycra consolidated an emerging sense of community, with a new twist. 'I didn't recognize you with your clothes on' was a common comment at the time among people who had been in the same exercise class when they encountered each other in other situations. The remark was often accompanied by nervous laughter. The humor arose from the fact that the comment implied a form of intimacy that was very different to the non-erotic physicality of aerobics. The nervousness arose from a shift in perception. On the street, conventional clothes seemed to detract from or disguise the 'real' person which Lycra had revealed in aerobics classes. Lycra's materiality – the *feeling* of Lycra, much commented on then and now, which simultaneously seemed to free the body and hold it, cover it and yet expose it – resonated on the level of felt experience. Wearing Lycra stimulated the new 'body consciousness' that was a core value of the millennial shift, across many different sectors. When Boomers talked to me about aerobics and their leggings more than twenty years later, their enthusiasm was undiminished. These four are representative:

> I came to it through dance, and I went on to teach aerobics. I was used to the ballet wear, but when Lycra came along it was wonderful, it never scrunched up like the old ballet kit. It fitted smoothly, like a skin, and it never moved up or slid down no matter what movements you did. Unlike the ballet clothes it was so shiny, it showed all the sweat. But that wasn't bad, in fact it was considered a 'plus'. You were *supposed* to sweat, and to show it.

> Leotards and leggings made me feel fitter, even just to put them on. It was the way they made your body *feel*, as though it was your own muscles that were holding you in, not something else.

Leggings and Lycra made you so aware of your body. Before, it was all about squeezing it in and covering it up. And with the clothes on top, no one could tell what you were really like. Then, everything changed, it was like you had nothing on. And the leggings and leotard would press against you, just that little bit. It was very sensual, it made you really *feel* your body, feel your self.

I was an exercise virgin. I'd never done anything like it before, or worn anything like it either. Lycra made you look as though you were proud of your body. I wasn't, but as soon as you put it on, the difference was amazing. *Nothing* wobbled. I still love Lycra. There should be a monument to Lycra.

Aerobics mania swept the nation, drawing in women who were coming to dance and exercise for the first time and creating a growing demand for aerobics wear that began to be filled by vanguard entrepreneurs like Gilda Marx, Jane Fonda and Debbie Moore of Pineapple Dance Studios, and then by many imitators. Marx was the first to come to Dupont's attention, when in 1976 she showed them a garment she had designed called a 'Flexatard', which she described as 'the perfect exercise suit – flexible, functional and fantastically glamorous', an outfit that would make women 'enjoy exercising even more'.[2] The Flexatard came in long-sleeved, cap-sleeve and spaghetti strap versions, in colors of sand, powder blue, roan, black, white, peach, lemon yellow, ink-green, raspberry and chocolate.

Marx's Flexatards were a harbinger. From made-to-order sources and small independent specialist shops, Lycra leggings and leotards began to edge toward the mainstream as aerobic exercise and associated cultural values and practices gained ground. This was also part of the 'millennial shift'. As Douglas noted, unbridled ecstasy

is a viable attitude only in the early, unorganized stages of a new movement. After the protest stage, once the need for organization is recognized, the negative attitude to rituals is seen to conflict with the need for a coherent system of expression. Then the ritualism reasserts itself around the new context of social relations.

(Douglas 1996: 20)

Ecstatic dance was transformed into 'disco', the informal studios of the early days gave way to the commercialized enterprises described by Maguire (2007), and Lycra itself became part of a new normativity of dress.

A *Dupont Fashion News* release of 1978 noted that Lycra was the perfect disco partner, made up into body-hugging pants and tube or tank tops to wear at

Studio 54 in New York, Annabel's in London or Regine's everywhere.[3] Initially, Dupont took little commercial interest in these developments. Compared to major foundation garment producers, ballet-wear manufacturers were small-scale customers, and Dupont made no direct sales to or profits from the individuals and small concerns who made the first aerobics leotards and leggings and disco wear from surplus foundation fabric. In any case, Dupont marketers still hoped that the slump in traditional foundations was just a passing fad, and that girdle-wearing would resume.

Dupont continued what it called its 'all out promotion' of 'Clothes Smoothers with Lycra', lightweight all-in-ones and other styles of foundations that were advertised as helping 'more and more women to look smoother, sleeker and more natural in their clothes'. Dupont promised their customers 'more consumer advertising, more in-store promotions, more coast-to-coast publicity' for what it now called 'innerwear', but the foundation market did not revive and there were other related problems for Dupont and the industry to deal with. With the death of the girdles that held them up, the sales of stockings – already in decline – plunged. The nylon pantyhose that were worn under miniskirts sagged and bagged at the knee, and the hosiery market did not rally until Dupont's 1979 introduction of pantyhose with Lycra, which kept their shape, revitalized the hosiery market.

As the 1980s began, Lycra leggings and leotards were in the studios, in the shops, on the streets – everywhere. Aerobic exercise videos and aerobic exercise books flooded the market, all showing women in Lycra. There was even a Workout Barbie doll, dressed in Lycra leggings, and a Barbie Workout video.

It was not until the early 1980s that Dupont took the aerobic-wear market seriously enough to conduct extensive market research into women's leotards. The first study[4] reported that leotards and leggings were the result of freedom of expression, which had emerged as a key value in American culture since the 1960s, and which had transformed attitudes to fitness, diet and clothing, citing examples such as the substitution of yoghurt for high-fat ice cream and the replacement of 'sneakers' by trainers and running shoes. In particular, the study found that the leotard and legging market had benefited from the popularity of aerobics, 'and in dance as a form of psychological release and expression', and also because it was no longer considered necessary to mask 'parts of the anatomy formerly hidden from view'. A second study[5] confirmed that Boomer women were the major buyers of leotards. In 1984, Americans purchased an estimated twenty-one million leotards worth $231 million at an average price of $10.90 for women aged fourteen and over, with 51 percent going to women between the ages of twenty-three and thirty-four. In the retail sector, Dupont's 1984 leotard study also established that the interest in exercise among American women, especially those of the Boomer cohort, were

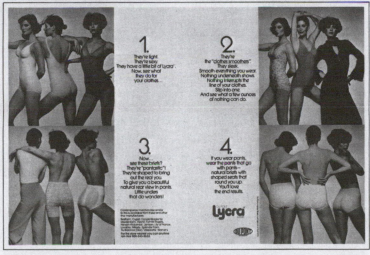

In 1977 Du Pont continues its all-out promotion behind Clothes Smoothers with Lycra.*

More consumer advertising, more in-store promotions. More coast-to-coast publicity. More sales coming up!

Send for Du Pont's plan for retail that will help rebuild, recapture and revamp your undergarment business. Send for it today. It's free! Write to Du Pont Company, Intimate Apparel, 350 Fifth Avenue, New York, N.Y. 10001.

*Du Pont registered trademark.

Figure 5.2 Lycra Clothes Smoothers, courtesy of Hagley Museum and Library.

creating new and growing markets for the leotard, beyond its use in aerobic, jazz dance and keep-fit exercise programs. First, halter-necked leotards were being used as beachwear by young women whose bodies had been made taut and lithe through exercise, replacing traditional boned and molded swimsuits. Second, the researchers detected a move by manufacturers to take the leotard look into other kinds of active sportswear including jogging, racquet sports and gym activities in which baggy clothes had long been customary. Third, the researchers found that leotards and dancewear were becoming acceptable as streetwear. Many new customers were not dancers, gymnasts or even exercisers, but they were attracted by the 'fashion look' of leotards worn with shorts, tops, short skirts and leg warmers.

A leader in this trend was Debbie Moore of Pineapple Dance Studios, London and New York, who had worked with Dupont to develop cotton/Lycra blends, which had taken over from shiny Antron/Lycra as the aerobic fabric of choice. Moore's (1983) *Pineapple Dance Book* had a formative effect on the aerobic dance movement, and her designs – the first ever outerwear using Lycra – transformed the clothing market. Already producing Pineapple dancewear, Moore was inspired by the way her dancers customized their street clothes. Looking at early cotton/Lycra samples – which had first been intended for use as underwear – she remembered thinking, she told me, 'Why not a little skirt? And then – why not wear leggings on the street?' She was the first to put street soles onto ballet pumps, launching the flatties that became *the* shoes for the look. She devised the double-fronted top, little Lycra tops with a double layer of supple supporting fabric so women didn't have to wear bras under them, and carried the design thinking on into dresses, skirts, crop trousers and tops, pioneering the layered look so you could wear several pieces together. Exemplifying fashion freedom, it struck a death blow to regimented dress categories and structured clothes, and women loved it. In 1982, *Women's Wear Daily* hailed Moore's designs as 'desk-to-dinner dressing', component-part clothing you could add to and subtract from throughout the day, just pausing to put on jewelry before going on the town for the night. Moore's was a completely new way of dressing that was based, as she says, on a combination of Lycra – 'the feel of the fabric, the fit and feel that are so important when it comes to fashion, the tactile-*ness*' and the Pineapple style and ethos. The Pineapple motto is 'survival of the fittest'.

The Dupont leotard marketing research report concluded that 'the current market strength is a legitimate reflection of consumer interest in fitness which we consider now to have become a permanent and fundamental influence on American life styles'.[6] In contrast to the foundation retailers polled by Dupont ten years earlier, American retailers of leotards, leggings and related goods were positive and their sales buoyant. Despite these promising reports, Dupont

Figure 5.3 The Pineapple Dance Book, courtesy of Debbie Moore.

did not pursue this new market energetically, although it passed on a summary of the report to their customers, in the usual way in a booklet entitled, *Leotards: Poised for Growth or Fashion Fad?* The 'increasingly self-confident, liberated woman of the "Me Generation"',[7] it reported, wanted to be included in a 'new mainstream' – the 'easy casual, minimal-dressing concept best expressed in the form of the leotard'. These women were dropping conventional items such as hats, gloves, spring coats, handkerchiefs and girdles, and opting for a 'less-is-more' style. They had probably bought their first leotards, body suits and leggings for exercise, but now thought it was 'OK' to wear them in public. 'Me Generation' women did not consider leotards a fad, but a new way to dress that was both functional and fashionable. Half of the sample polled owned three or more; and of these, 20 percent owned five or more. After imparting this information, the booklet did not make the usual elaborate suggestions for marketing, merely suggesting that store promotions built around fitness might stimulate sales. By 1986, a survey circulated at Dupont reported that exercise garments were 'going and growing', with 60 percent of adult women being regular exercisers, 36 million of them aerobics participants.[8] But, although the sales of stretch fiber to leotard and sportswear makers had reached substantial proportions and would continue to rise, Dupont never developed the close relationship with leotards and leggings that it had with the girdle.

Possibly, like the loss of the gunpowder market long ago, the collapse of the girdle market forced Dupont to extend Lycra's range faster and wider than they might otherwise have done. From sock tops, knitted cuffs, waistbands and belts, Lycra was soon extended into swimwear that didn't sag when wet, children's clothing with freedom of movement, knitwear that held its shape, blouses and skirts that didn't need darts or tailoring for shaping, trousers that didn't bag at the knees and jackets that didn't bag at the elbows. Dupont's cultural production continued, because, although they were not inventing new fibers at the same rate, they were developing new uses for existing fibers, which had to be promoted to retailers and consumers. To educate about the advantages of clothes containing Lycra, Dupont created the 'Stretch Corps', a mobile field force of 120 trained men and women. Dressed in uniforms of burgundy jackets with white shirts and smart trousers or slim skirts fashioned from fabrics of Lycra blends, they toured stores throughout the country, demonstrating new ways of selling stretch to customers.[9] Instead of control, the focus was on function, and on the way that Lycra, when mixed with Dupont's other fibers, could help the working woman to meet the challenges of her life. Women were moving out into the working world in their numbers, 38,500,000 in 1978, and Dupont's fibers, as a press release put it, were designed 'for *real women* who live full, sixteen hour days, not on showroom runways, at balls and three hour lunches, but in and out of offices, supermarkets, PTA meetings, cars and subways'.[10]

There were fashion shows, demonstrations, promotions, swingtags, sponsorships, television commercials and a steady flow of press releases. Dupont provided retailers with sales training videos and in-store video films, among them *Ms Liz Goes Shopping With Mom*. Made in 1982 to help retailers sell the new Lycra panties, it was a humorous cartoon that reflected new trends in society and in retailing. There are no more star foundation salesgirls like Selma in the video because the shops are now mainly self-service, and it is Ms – not Miss – Liz who makes the decisions, and keeps Mom up to date: 'Liz: Since I started wearing panties with Lycra, I won't wear anything less. And Steve thinks they look great, too![11] Mom: She really knows how to break a mother's heart!' Thanks to Dupont's efforts, 'stretch' became an essential quality in clothes of all kinds, something consumers now expected and took for granted. A 'need' had been both created and filled, and in the process new meanings and associations became attached to Lycra. While the fiber had symbolized constraint when used in a girdle, and freedom when used in leggings and leotards, Dupont's periodic 'Awareness Surveys' carried out to monitor product recognition among consumers revealed that Lycra had now become associated with 'comfort'. It was an association that arose from the material qualities of the fiber, and harmonized with the mood and mores of the time across all sectors of the consumer market. From then on, the company actively promoted it in its advertising, with phrases like 'comfort magic', 'hours of comfort', 'beauty and comfort', 'performance and comfort' and 'nothing more comfortable'.

Despite its success in these new fields, Dupont periodically revisited the possibility of reviving the girdle. The 'Jeangirdle' never materialized, and jeans continued to present the company with a challenge, because young Boomer women wore them in preference to skirts or dresses, which required hosiery and, formerly, girdles. Beginning in 1977, Dupont carried out several studies of the young female jean-buying population, striving to 'build a better mousetrap',[12] alluding to the phrase attributed to Ralph Waldo Emerson: 'Build a better mousetrap and the world will beat a path to your door.' Finally, improvements in fiber blends led to the development of what became the highly popular denim jeans with Lycra, which gave good fit and comfort but did not look like stretch jeans:[13] wearers did not have to worry about being 'found out'. Lycra panties, control top pantyhose and support pantyhose hadn't existed when the Boomers first gave up the girdle: the company wondered if Boomer women could be induced to wear them now, thereby creating a kind of girdle market in disguise. However, research carried out in 1982 found that the very word 'control' was still problematic. As the report noted: 'To many women this word says "girdle" and unequivocally many potential users have been dissuaded because of this word.'[14] In the expansive years that followed the heyday of the legging, Lycra exceeded all the company's original expectations, ultimately becoming one of the most profitable of all Dupont products (Hounshell and Smith 1988b: 431). Progress was steady, efficient and discreet. Almost ten years passed before Lycra again took a prominent place on the public stage, during which time substantial changes took place inside and outside Dupont's Textile Division.

During the 1980s and into the 1990s, fiber development at Dupont underwent a shift in market focus (Crippen *et al.* 1995), resulting in a privileging of development over research. Instead of the mass market which had long been their forte, Dupont now aimed to target niche markets with specialty fibers, which required a fundamental shift in marketing techniques. From the beginning of the company, 'Dupont' had been the one over-arching brand and identity, but now a different style of management and marketing was introduced under which chosen products would acquire more high-profile, individual identities. Lycra became a 'global brand', split into four regions – Europe, North America, South America and Asia Pacific. Within each Lycra region, individual managers were responsible for different special categories of Lycra application such as hosiery, active sportswear, intimate apparel and ready-to-wear. Classic leotards and leggings were not considered by Dupont to fall into any of these categories, at least no one I encountered wanted to claim responsibility for them.

Company documents on the reasons for the shift remain sealed under in-house confidentiality regulations, but in the case of Lycra an important factor would have been the rise in synthetic-fiber production by competitors at home and abroad, particularly in the Asia Pacific region, after Dupont had had the stretch market more or less to itself for some twenty years. Although inferior to Dupont's fibers, the rival products could supply a level of performance acceptable to the mass market at cheaper prices, obliging Dupont to apply their premium-products-at-premium-prices rule to increasingly specialized segments of the market where high-performance fibers were valued, such as active sport. The future of Lycra, one Dupont director said, would lie in 'constantly finding new markets, new uses'.[15] Another factor was that, with increasing globalization, the need for a strong international brand image was felt. Instead of independent advertising agencies in different countries, Dupont began to work with single multinational agencies who could provide global coverage. The Textile Fibers Division was streamlined and reorganized, and between 1990 and 1995 Dupont spent $5 billion strengthening and improving all aspects of Lycra, 'right down to its molecular structure'.[16] Thanks to the company's sustained promotional efforts over many years, brand recognition was already very high, and Lycra was overwhelmingly associated with 'comfort' and 'stretch' in the public mind, but it was now thought necessary to move beyond this, to associate Lycra with something more than function, and this something turned out to be fashion.

The new key concept became 'movement', especially 'freedom of movement'. In 1994, a Lycra symbol or logo was created – the triangular Lycra 'wave' – an easily recognizable image that was chosen to convey 'movement'.

Like the original Dupont oval, it was intended to serve as a mark of quality for the assurance of manufacturers and customers, and it was put onto labels and garment tags. Lycra now went high profile. Dupont courted the fashion industry assiduously, securing endorsements for Lycra from designers like Giorgio Armani, Donna Karan and Gianni Versace, showing their designs in advertisements run in top fashion magazines, newspapers and on television. From the very beginning, a besetting challenge for Lycra was that it was invisible. As an ingredient brand, it never appeared on its own, but was used to give stretch to other fibers, like nylon and cotton. In basic mass-market clothing, functional performance was the ultimate test of a fiber, but in fashion as the 1952 Dress Survey had noted, appearance was what mattered. Dupont had to make an invisible difference visible, and the most dramatic way to do this was to promote the body-hugging clothes beloved of the supermodels of the day, exemplified by the designs of Azzedine Alaia, nicknamed 'the King of Cling'.

In a pioneering example of creating a uniform global message for a product, the advertising campaign 'Nothing Moves Like Lycra' was devised and tested simultaneously in eleven countries before it was released. The models in the campaign had been chosen for their 'international' look and 'everyday' appeal that would be 'translatable across Europe, Asia and South America'.[17] Dupont began to sponsor high-profile events like designer fashion fairs and awards and catwalk shows, associating the company with cutting-edge style nationally and internationally. Subsequent waves of up-market advertising reinforced the new Lycra image. 'Sport is the new religion' was a catchphrase of the time, and Lycra took full advantage, using the 1996 Olympics as an opportunity to showcase its new high-performance sports fibers, *Dupont Magazine* noting, 'It is said that every medal winner in every Olympic sport has some Du Pont Lycra brand spandex in at least one item of apparel.'[18]

By 1998, Lycra numbered eighth in Interbrand's list of the world's top textile brands. Starting at the top, the ten were Levi's, Nike, Adidas, Reebok, Chanel, Benetton, Armani, Lycra, Wrangler and Hugo Boss. And in 1999, Lycra was selected as one of the top fashion innovations of the twentieth century by the Council of Fashion Designers of America. Listed as number fourteen out of a total of twenty-five, Lycra was also an ingredient in many of the other entries, some of which were also Dupont innovations. The full list was:

1) Wash-and-wear fabric. 2) Online Shopping. 3) Luggage On Wheels. 4) The Bikini. 5) Pants for Women. 6) Denim. 7) Casual Fridays. 8) The Push-Up Bra. 9) The Little Black Dress. 10) The Hippie Look. 11) The Credit Card. 12) The Pantyhose. 13) Separates. 14) Lycra. 15) Ralph Lauren. 16) Polyester. 17) The Cotton T-Shirt. 18) The Backpack. 19) Khakis. 20) The Dryer. 21) The Mini-skirt. 22) Giorgio Armani. 23) The Disco Look. 24) The Sports Bra. 25) The Preppy Look.[19]

With the year 2000 looming, Dupont joined the wave of global enthusiasm for the Millennium, seeking to use it as a means of promoting Lycra as a future-oriented, innovation-seeking, fashion-minded brand. It embarked upon cultural production by sponsoring a lavishly illustrated book, *Millennium Mode* (Wolf and Schlachter 2000) featuring futuristic fashion designs and predictions from forty designers and labels such as Prada, Missoni and Issey Miyake.

In 1998, a Dupont employee had told me, 'Lycra is coming up to its fortieth birthday but we are playing it down.' In 1947, Dupont had been proud to boast that theirs was 'A Heritage 145 Years Young',[20] but in 2000 it was not thought desirable for Lycra to appear to be middle-aged. Nonetheless, as part of their Millennium celebrations, Dupont decided to celebrate Lycra's fortieth birthday, one year late. The anniversary was marked by promotions at industry events such as the 'Material World' trade show, where Dupont, their customers and their customers' customers heard fashion luminaries like Tommy Hilfiger, Jean-Paul Gaultier and Betsy Johnson heap praise upon Lycra, the latter enthusing: 'Happy Birthday Lycra! We love you! We love you!'[21]

The then Global Brand Manager of Dupont Lycra noted with satisfaction: 'When we do consumer research, the kinds of words they use to describe Lycra are: healthy and active, spirited and attractive, modern, sexy, innovative. All pretty nice qualities to be associated with a forty year old brand.'[22] Boomer women would no doubt describe themselves in the same way, but Dupont's birthday celebrations were not aimed at Lycra's fellow 'fortysomethings', the Boomers. Instead, Dupont was beginning to target what had been identified as Lycra's new market – the teenagers of Generation Y; children and grandchildren of the Boomers, readers of new magazines like *Teen Vogue* and *Cosmo Girl*.[23]

In that Millennium summer, there was another significant 'birthday'. Some 3,000 recognized descendants of the patriarch Pierre Samuel du Pont were invited by the Dupont family history organization to attend a family reunion in Wilmington to celebrate the two-hundredth anniversary of the arrival of the family in America. The event was marked by an exhibition at the Brandywine Museum of Art entitled *The duPont family – 200 Years of Portraits*. Among recently executed portraits of family members in the sixth or seventh generation of descent from the patriarch, many showed the distinctive Dupont nose and dimpled chin. They no longer lived together on the Brandywine, but the sense of family – and, literally, its face – was still strong. Relations between company and family had altered. The family no longer directed the day-to-day running of the company, although they retained substantial stock holdings in it. However, in the public culture of the company – brochures, publications and on the website – the family heritage continued to feature prominently.

Lycra, Dupont and the Boomers, Second Time Around

Dupont was targeting youth, but the decision to do so was not unanimous. The difference of opinion within the Textile Division about whether more should be done for existing customers, including the Boomers, or whether marketing should develop in a new direction, had been ongoing, but the latter view had now prevailed. I also observed that Dupont were becoming more guarded about their fiber activities in general, less willing to disclose their future plans.

Dupont set up a teenage website, sponsored youth TV shows like *California Summer Countdown*,[24] organized teenage focus groups, revitalized their involvement with denim and partnered with Levi Strauss and Company to introduce Lycra in their new misses, juniors and girls lines,[25] promoted Lycra in youth publications like *Glamour, Lucky* and *Cosmo Girl*, and mounted Lycra teen retail promotions incorporating rock music performances with role models like R&B artist Kelis, reminiscent of the campaigns it had mounted long ago for the first 'teenage' Boomers.

Their new Lycra marketing campaign – themed *Enjoy the Difference* – focused on children and teenagers wearing the baggy gear and backwards baseball caps favored by the slacker cohorts, but made with Lycra. Following established procedure, Dupont had done their market research, and the company shared their findings on the Lycra teen website:

As America's teen population grows at twice the rate of the adult population, to an estimated 35 million girls and boys by 2010, teens are wielding some considerable power to influence the retail marketplace. What they earn, what they spend, and what they think is 'cool' or not will make a concrete impact on the bottom line at major retailers…. The spending power of Generation Y is projected to skyrocket into the next century…. *Women's Wear Daily* says 'they are one of the greatest opportunities in the population. If you build a market with teens, they'll build your business into the 21st century.'[26]

That's what Dupont had said about the Boomers, the first youth consumers, back in 1965. So – where were those Boomers and the leggings they wanted now?

Figure 5.4 'Move It, Shake It, Mix It Up. With Lycra', author's collection.

Figure 5.5 Lycra Sportivement, author's collection.

From my first contact with the company, I had encountered deep-seated corporate resistance to associating Dupont and Lycra with the 1980s and aerobic leggings. 'We've done a lot since then' I was told firmly, on several occasions. In 1998, Dupont mounted a feature on their website that asked, 'Do you think of Lycra as a material of the 1980s?' before going on to describe Lycra's subsequent development in detail.[27]

By 2002, new market research showed that 98 percent of people polled 'recognized' the name Lycra, and associated it with stretch and comfort. But what the poll did *not* reveal was what my research turned up consistently – that among the general public above the age of thirty and quite a lot of younger people, Lycra was identified with a particular garment – the leggings – and a particular period, the 1980s, these being two of many near-identical field responses:

In the 1980s it was all big hair, Dynasty and Dallas, and Lycra went with all of that. It was a glamorous look, all matching leotards, sweatbands, leg-warmers, ladies in Lycra.

Leggings were the thing in the 1980s. They were real shiny and in garish colors, you don't see that shiny Lycra or those colors any more. And there were lots of long black ones too. That was all part of women in aerobics classes. Upbeat types, wannabes. Definitely there was energy there, a lot of energy. People were always talking about energy, and walking around in Lycra, not only in the gym.

These were associations from which Dupont struggled to escape, posting features like this on the Lycra website:

Remember how Lycra used to be less cool than a jumper knitted by your Gran? Well, the likes of Julian McDonald and a host of other world class designers have been using the material most associated with fluorescent aerobics instructors in abundance in their latest collections.[28]

But escape seemed impossible. Lycra had been a defining part of the popular culture of the period, coming to symbolize the late 1970s and the 1980s so completely that it seemed entirely appropriate that the 1999 hit stage musical *Mama Mia*, a celebration of the songs of the disco-era pop group ABBA, begins with the following announcement as the house lights are dimmed: 'Members of the audience are warned that white Lycra will be worn at this performance.'

Inevitably, this identification with an era meant identification with the dominant cohort of that era, the Boomers, as expressed in the statement I heard so many times during fieldwork when I asked members of Generations X and Y about Lycra leggings: 'That's what my mother wore.'

So closely identified with a specific era and cohort, it was inevitable that Lycra, leggings and aerobics would find themselves used as a negative sign in the discourse of generational difference, a symbol of the growing tensions between 'young' and 'old'. The edge I had felt in some early retail field responses found material expression in a window display I spotted in a flag-ship shop of a transnational brand favored by young slackers. Store window displays are an under-analyzed form of public culture, the retail equivalent of the mediating activity performed by magazines. No longer simple displays of goods for sale, the most advanced are considered by their creators to be 'statements' that mix commerce and culture. 'We don't just dump stuff in the window, our displays *say* something,' one Creative Display Manager told me, while another said, 'It's our job to put together the mood, the message and the "look" that sell the clothes. Sometimes we don't even use the clothes.' The window in question was an ironic deconstruction of the fitness movement of the 1980s. The background was a montage of pages ripped out of publications like *Jane Fonda's Workout Book*, all showing young lithe Boomers in Lycra leotards and leggings, surrounding a central panel of photographs of a very plump model, cavorting in loose and baggy casual clothes. In front of the montage was a stationary exercise bicycle, its seat covered with frivolous pink marabou. Into the bicycle stirrups a pair of fluffy pink bedroom slippers had been inserted instead of athletic trainers. Mounted on the handlebars was a wicker basket full of packaging from fat-tening foods like potato chips, cookies and pizza. Oversized pill bottles labeled 'Stop Dieting' lay on the floor and, in the foreground, was a big garbage can full of the best-selling aerobic videos of the 1980s by people like Jane Fonda and Cher, the tapes unraveled and spilling out onto the floor. 'What's this window about?' I asked. 'It's our new collection,' replied the shop person.

> It's saying, 'You don't need to exercise to look good and be cool.' That kind of exercise isn't cool any more. It's over. Now it's all about fun. To look good and be cool and have fun, all you have to do is buy our clothes.

I saw something more in the window display – anti-ageism symbolized through Lycra and discarded aerobic exercise videos. It reminded me of ritual ancestor killing, familiar to early anthropologists as part of age-grade initiation ceremonies, where young initiates ritually 'killed' their elders, signifying they were now taking their place. So pervasive was this negative association of age and aerobic leggings that toward the end of fieldwork I began to find Boomers themselves rejecting them. Sometimes this was an enforced change: 'After all these years, they finally wore out and I couldn't find new ones to buy.' For others, it was a conscious choice: 'I realized I had started to look old-fashioned,' said one, while another told me, 'It's such a stereotype now, isn't it? I don't want to look like I'm stuck in a time warp.' One Boomer who had been exercising in old Lycra leotards for years turned up to her AOA class in slacker-style combat trousers saying: 'I never thought I'd do this, but I feel so up-to-date in them. I feel younger.'

However, these women were in the minority. Many Boomers who had drifted away from exercise as they took on family and work commitments and grew older were now returning to the gym for health reasons like the Boomer woman of the ethnographic moment, and like her they wanted the leotards and leggings they associated with their youth. In the decade between 1983 and 1993, the number of American adults who said they exercised vigorously rose from 34 percent to 40 percent[29] and the figures were rising steadily. But other Boomers were heading in another direction – to the shops. In the Boomer age group, the sole category of apparel with Lycra that was showing rising sales was 'shapewear'.

The trend had been spotted as early as 1995, when designer Nancy Ganz, trying on a tight-fitting outfit at Bloomingdales, thought, 'If only I could put Lycra in these clothes.'[30] Seeing a market opportunity, she went on to found a company that produced Lycra foundation garments with names like 'Hipslip' that shaped the body in order to make the clothes look better. These found ready buyers among Boomers, of whom the editor of the *American Marketing to Women* newsletter said, 'The majority want to fight sagging and will do almost anything to do so.'[31] Ganz was the first of many to move into this market gap. 'It's a runaway success,'[32] said the Public Relations manager for lingerie chain Victoria's Secret, referring to the sales of shaping foundation garments which *Women's Wear Daily* reported were being bought by aging Boomers. Vassarette had developed a new UnderShapers line for Boomers, the Product Manager explained, 'Because this consumer is a little different, she's not as old in her mind as she really is. She would just like to wear her pretty panties, but she needs more control.'[33] Manufacturers and retailers were pleased with the sales surge but also cautious – many now in senior positions remembered the death of the girdle. 'People are willing to try control bottoms as long as they're not called girdles. They look more like daywear, not like the "G" word,'[34] said the Vice President of Merchandising at True Form. 'Nobody says the g-word anymore,' said the Divisional Vice President of Intimate Apparel in a major group of department stores.[35]

The superior technological qualities of Lycra made it the manufacturer's choice for these demanding garments which required the high performance level that budget stretch fibers could not deliver. Dupont took advantage of these new developments, announcing in a press release:

> **Thanks to Lycra Soft Shaping, there's no longer any need to suffer in the name of beauty.** Today, some 50% of the female population in Western Europe are over 50 years of age … also the percentage of single women is on the rise and their hectic lifestyles don't always give them enough time to look after their bodies as much as they would like. However these women want to stay young longer, to continue to be attractive, and need to feel self-confident in all situations. Garments designed to flatten the tummy and push-up the buttocks and bras to shape the bust make it possible for women to mask their little 'imperfections' – but, above all they want to look good with no restraints. In response to the ever-increasing number of women seeking body-firming control that contours, slims and imparts confidence without sacrificing comfort, femininity and fashion, Dupont has created Lycra Soft.[36]

On its website, Dupont reported that one of its customers, a shapewear company called 'Lipo in a Box', had sold out its entire run of Long Leg Brief shapers in just six minutes on the America QVC shopping channel. 'Shapers' may have seemed like a revolution in foundation wear – but they were not new. In another ironic twist, 'shapewear' was essentially the 'Clothes Smoothers' that Dupont and the manufacturers had promoted so energetically in the 1970s, in an effort to save the girdle, and which had been resoundingly rejected by the young Boomers. Now, some twenty-five years later, when time and gravity had done their work, the Boomers and the girdle had finally caught up with each other. The style of the foundations, the promotional phrases, the very names of the garments were virtually identical. Only, this time, vanguard fifty-something Boomers no longer considered foundations 'deceitful', and 'control' was no longer a dirty word. Finally, the song 'A Shape is a Woman', which had been written in 1975 for Dupont to use in promoting 'Form Persuaders' to Boomers, seemed to fit:

> A shape is a natural thing
> A shape is freedom to be what you are
> What you want to be
> A shape is what everyone sees
> In you.[37]

The Boomers, however, did not see Shapers as girdles or foundation garments. 'It's just like wearing leotards and leggings' was a frequent comment. As in the

1970s, what was virtually the identical garment was being seen completely differently by consumers and producers.

Although their faith in foundation garments had been proved right in the end, Dupont did little to associate themselves with this new market surge, apart from cautioning in *Dupont Magazine*: 'Shhh ... don't use the "g-word" ... to girdle is to slice a tree's bark and choke off its life blood. Call these up-to-date underpinnings shapewear.'[38] And there was no rapprochement between Dupont and the Boomer cohort that had rejected the girdle. Dupont kept their public distance from the Boomers, and in the company's promotional activities, it was teen and youthwear that received attention, not the Boomer-oriented shapewear.

Tellingly, in 2000, Dupont had issued a mythic narrative about Lycra in the form of a revealing timeline, widely circulated to the press, that highlighted the fiber's contribution to the past, present and future of fashion. Like all timelines, it consisted of a schematic presentation of key events and achievements in chronological order.

Beginning with 'Imagine life without Lycra? We can't. Because Lycra is irreplaceable.... Life without Lycra? Now, that's a real stretch',[39] the timeline started with the discovery of 'Fiber K'. The next year, 1959, is illustrated with a tiny picture of a girdle and a caption that reads: 'Smooth move. Lycra replaces rubber in corsets for a more natural, more comfortable look.' The word 'girdle' is not used. 1960 is hailed as the year the benefits of lightweight fabrics with Lycra were recognized worldwide. Then comes 1962, the year that Lycra was first used in support hose. The next year on the timeline is 1974, when Lycra was first used in swimwear, followed by 1979 when Lycra was first used in pantyhose. The 1980s are represented by a single entry for 1985, when Lycra 'became standard equipment for athletes like basketball's Michael Jordan and tennis champ Andre Agassi and a new street look is born'.

The next entry on the timeline, 1993, is the beginning of the new reorganized Lycra division. From then on, every year has its own caption, detailing the introduction of 'Lycra Soft' fibers, 'Lycra Power' compression shorts, Wool Plus Lycra for use in men's suiting, shoes with Lycra, leather with Lycra, and a Lycra website for consumers the world over. The Lycra timeline was notable not for what it showed, but for what it did not show. Leggings and leotards do not appear, and the troublesome 1980s that saw the death of the girdle and the rise of the legging were effectively left off, as if they had never happened.

There are several possibilities for this omission. The most obvious is 'organizational embarrassment' over an uncharacteristic setback, although ultimately Lycra leotards and leggings were not a failure for Dupont, but rather a stage in the resoundingly successful development of Lycra as a whole. Another possibility is what has been called 'institutional amnesia' (Pollitt 2000), the fact

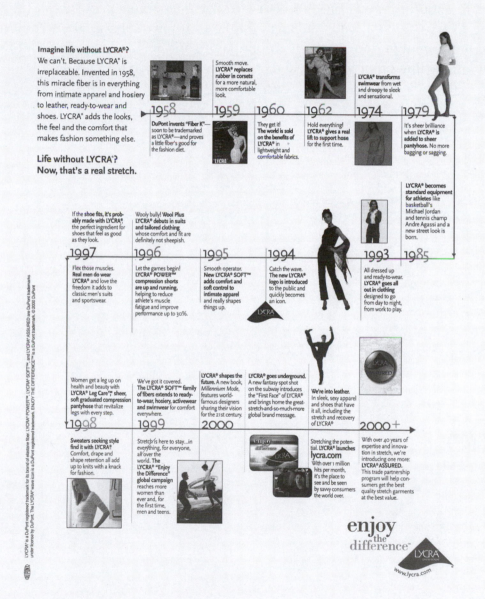

Figure 5.6 Lycra timeline, author's collection.

that in our overloaded information age it is simply not possible to 'remember' everything – but this is unlikely, particularly since the public remembered Lycra leggings and leotards very clearly. The final possibility was that there was something about the cultural values, meanings and associations linked to leotards and leggings that Dupont wanted to escape, that explains their absence from the timeline and, as my Boomer woman shopper of the ethnographic moment had found, from the shops. But what were these negative values? I thought about Lycra's delayed fortieth birthday, corporate unease about Lycra being seen as 'middle aged', the focus on the youth market even though there were more midlife Boomers in the population, and realized that the cultural values impacting on production and consumption as seen through Lycra must have to do with 'age'.

6

ANOTHER ETHNOGRAPHIC
MOMENT

I was at Hagley when Dupont announced that they were selling the Textile Division, and Lycra with it. A palpable sense of shock hung in the air. I now realized why the company had become reticent about its future plans. The local newspaper ran guarded expressions of regret from retired senior employees, many of whom had worked their way up through the Textile Division in its glory days. No one wanted to say much. Like trouble in the family, it was best kept private. The company had now diversified into new areas such as life sciences[1] and, despite Dupont's efforts, the textile market as a whole had not been buoyant. A flood into the market of cheaper imported fibers from non-Western producers and a sharp rise in the cost of raw materials were the reasons given for the decision, and Dupont stock rose as soon as the announcement was made. It was hoped that, under a new owner, the Textile Division could flourish.[2] As a stand-alone unit, it was the largest integrated textile fiber and interiors company in the world, with an annual revenue of $6.5 billion and 22,000 employees, operating in fifty countries.[3] However, after so long, separation from the parent company seemed hard to many who had been directly involved. 'Textiles have been losing money lately,' one Dupont retiree said to me softly, shaking his head, 'but I didn't think it would come to this.' For this man, who had worked on Lycra for the whole of his professional career, it was a bitter thing. I walked past the silent powder mills, down to the Brandywine. How, I wondered, *had* it come to this? And what was *this*?

The analysis had begun with one ethnographic moment, and it would now end with another. The narratives of the Dupont family and firm seemed preternaturally present, embedded in the landscapes around me – the Hagley site now, and as it had once been, the Pontiana of the physiocrats. I looked up to the old Dupont family home and the small office with its floor worn away by generations of Duponts, where plans were devised that led to the first products that carried the family name and built the family powder company that went on to create the synthetic fiber industry. Facing it, on a bluff overlooking the Brandywine, was the Pioneering Research Laboratory where Lycra had been developed and continually refined. I thought about the men and women at the Waynesboro Works, about Selma the Star Sales Girl, and the Brain-stormers, many of whose wildest suggestions for Lycra had materialized.

I saw how Lycra had come into being, and had acquired different meanings and associations that had come to define different people in different times and places, socially, locally and globally. And how Lycra had shaped social and physical bodies, and been shaped by them in return. All around me were the roots of the 'strong company culture', imbued with the ethos of 'family' and the tradition of research that had been responsible for the creation of so much of the stuff that made up our everyday material world. *Fiber Facts* had been justifiably proud of 'bigness'; nothing before or since has rivaled the achievements of Dupont's Textile Fibers Division in creating, developing and establishing fibers that changed the way people lived.

That year – 2002 – was the Dupont bicentenary, commemorating the two-hundredth anniversary of the founding of the company. The year-long cele-bration included the setting up of a special bicentenary website, the publication of a new authorized company history, *Dupont: From the Banks of the Brandywine to Miracles of Science* (Kinnane 2002), and many commemora-tive events which focused on the family and the company's early years, con-sciously harking back to its heritage and its historic mission of innovation, demonstrating the consolidating power of myth, as strong in the present as in the past.

But this had come too late for the Textile Division and Lycra. It was now clear that in the cyclical trends of the 1980s and 1990s, the sacrifice of research to development in pursuit of cost reductions and reorganization into strategic business units (McMillan and Hicks 2001) may have gone too far for textiles. In recent years the focus had been on finding new ways to spin Lycra, not on inventing a new Lycra. Some people within the company had foreseen the pos-sible dangers, particularly 'old hands'. One retired Pioneering Research sci-entist explained it by drawing me a diagram, of the sort scientists and doctors love to use when talking to a layperson: a sunburst, with rays stretching out in every direction from a central circle.

> This is how we used to do it. Inside that circle in the middle there would be an idea, a question, like 'moisture' or 'stretch'. And we'd work on it every which way, everything it could mean, every kind of fiber that solved the problem. That's what all those lines going out from the center are – all the answers to the question, all different kinds of fibers and processes. In the end, only a few were used, maybe only two or three, but the rest of it was there, for when we might need it. And we often did, even years later. We were ready, the work was done, all we had to do was get it on the road. No more.

He drew a thin wedge into the circle, like cutting a small slice of pie.

> That's how they do it now. Focused, they call it. In our research, we had no limits, we didn't know what we were going to find, and that's how we made new discoveries. Now they tell them what to find, they find it and that's all. Sure, it's cheaper now, but not in the long run.

He stabbed his pencil at all the lines still left outside the wedge. 'They won't have any new ideas in the bank, like we did. One day the well is going to run dry.' And according to local reactions that emerged when the shock of the announcement wore off, that's what a lot of people thought had happened.

By 2002, the year of the announcement, only 20 percent of the company's revenue came from products less than five years old, a telling proportion for a companion associated with innovation, which had been reflected in a decline in Dupont's stock price since 1998.[4] Not only analysts, but many Dupont employees blamed the abandoning of the core research culture for the present difficulties.[5] To counteract this negative publicity, Dupont publicly declared a new commitment to research, although in new areas like the life sciences, not the chemistry on which their textile work had been based. From this perspective, instead of being simply a solution to a loss-making situation, the projected sale of the Textile Division was seen by some observers[6] as a symbolic act, an indication that the company was turning the page and moving forward into a new age of innovation. But it was difficult for many of the old Lycra hands to see it that way.

For others – particularly members of the Lycra marketing and management team – it would be an end and a beginning. Some would leave the company, others would move on to join the eventual purchaser of the hived-off division, and Lycra itself would be uprooted from Wilmington, its ancestral soil. Could these changes have been avoided if different choices had been made, and Dupont had concentrated on the large and loyal Boomer cohort who had the income and – to use a core company concept – 'need' for premium fibers at premium prices? The question hung over Hagley that day, unspoken and unanswerable.

And I thought about the Boomers – the cohort for whom Lycra had been created, who wore the first toddlers' clothes with stretch, and grew up to buy pantyhose with Lycra that didn't bag at the knees, swimsuits with Lycra that didn't sag when they got wet and leggings of Lycra to work out in. The same Boomers who – although they were still the largest cohort in the population, with the largest disposable income – now had trouble finding 'stuff for us'. But who and what made the Generation Y youth market so attractive to Dupont? The surprising answer, I concluded, was – the Boomers themselves.

Dupont were not the only company who seemed to be ignoring the aging Boomers. Market observers of all kinds had been mystified by the failure of the commercial market for older boomers to materialize, as expected. Since they were infants, Boomers had set off waves of production and consumption, generating an unprecedented deluge of innovative 'stuff' created especially for them. It was assumed that the Boomers would go on in the same way for the rest of their lives, setting off new cohort-specific production imperatives, but they hadn't. Between 'young' stuff and geriatric goods there was a vast gray area – actually not gray, since gray hair was no longer a common sight, and older people no longer habitually wore gray as they once had. One place where Boomers had continued to drive innovation in the marketplace was in anti-aging products and services such as hair dye, face creams, cosmetic surgery and dentistry and Viagra, but other areas of the market that once served older consumers had disappeared completely. 'Dressing appropriately for one's age' had been one of the essential criteria of self-confidence in Dupont's 'Self Confidence' survey of 1959, but all that had been swept away in the youthquake of the 1960s. Now people refused to dress in a certain way just because of their age, and it went beyond that: the youth-loving Boomers simply refused to get old. In the 1940s, the fortieth birthday was the beginning of middle age (Brandes 1985), but as the Boomer cohort aged, they began to move the goalposts. Fifty became the new forty, and as the vanguard Boomers grew older, sixty became the new fifty. Finally, the Boomers abandoned chronological definitions of age altogether in favor of an indefinite 'midlife' that stretches to the grave. In the market, this was reflected in the absence of goods for older Boomers – and the failure of most such goods that did appear. Boomers, it seemed, did not want to define themselves as old by buying stuff designed and made for old people. But 'old stuff' in the sense of the stuff of their youth was different – as witnessed by the booming market for vintage goods on eBay, and my Boomer shopper of the ethnographic moment, looking for Lycra leggings like she 'used to have'.

In the world of public culture, this was clearly seen in women's magazines, with which the promotion of Lycra had been so closely involved in the early days. Just as the postwar baby boom drove the production of baby products, then toys and then children's clothes as the Boomers grew up, so magazine publishers responded to the opening of this new market by launching new magazines for children, then subteens and teenagers, and finally in the 1960s, magazines for what was then called the 'New Woman'. New social categories and values had been objectified in new magazines. However, in the 1980s, this had begun to break down. Despite the fact that the Boomer cohort was aging, the target readership for women's magazines became frozen at about the age of thirty-five and had remained so. Boomer women complained to me about adult fashion magazines with sixteen-year-old girls on the cover and 'unsuitable' clothes inside, deploring the lack of age-appropriate 'magazines for us'. Yet women's magazines aimed specifically at the older market had not succeeded. As one magazine publisher and former fashion editor who had decided not to enter this field, a Boomer herself, told me:

> You have to be very careful in that market, and I would not touch it with a bargepole. One of the problems is that, as a consumer, I am unlikely to bound up to the newsstand and say 'Hurrah, here is something for the older woman!' because in my mind I am not an older woman. And advertisers are a big problem in this market. Advertisers don't want to tarnish their image as a brand by associating with older people.

A managing director of one of the world's leading lifestyle and fashion magazine publishers told me much the same thing:

> Magazines for the older women – I have a colleague who buttonholes me about this every time we're alone together in the elevator. It seems like it should work. But you know, what people say they want and what they actually *do* want are very different. We hear people say they want more mature models on the cover and inside the magazine, and more pictures of 'real' people in 'real' clothes. We hear and we listen. But three times now, we've put older models on the cover, and each time the circulation dipped. When we put pictures of quite ordinary clothes inside, readers write in and complain. So we have concluded that, whatever they say, our readers don't really want this. We aren't alone in this view. Magazines that have set out to cater for the older women are no longer with us.

The problem of Boomer resistance to seeing themselves as old or being seen as 'older' by others was not confined to fashion magazines. The magazine with the largest circulation in America is published by AARP, the American Association of Retired Persons. An invitation to join AARP is sent to Americans on their fiftieth birthday. 'How did they find out?' is a common Boomer reaction. AARP has an affordable annual subscription and a range of services for members including financial planning, investment advice, health insurance and a monthly magazine, *Modern Maturity*.

By 2000, with Boomers in their numbers becoming eligible to join AARP, the look of the magazine needed updating but AARP also felt it had to address the problems of size and cohort difference represented by the Boomers, who were seen by the publishers of *Modern Maturity* as 'a unique club, one whose members feel a special affinity toward one another based on a shared history and culture' (Bercovici 2003: 1). Readership surveys indicated that Boomers wanted a magazine of their own, and in 2001 AARP launched *My Generation*, for Boomer members. *My Generation* was not about being old, it was about getting there – and having fun along the way. It included features that encouraged Boomers to take their holidays at Graceland or to drive down Route 66, on how even the cartoon character Dennis the Menace was fifty, on how important it was to exercise, in an article entitled 'Use It or Lose It'. 'There's really no magazine that talks to men and women of the baby-boomer generation, but *My Generation* will change all that' (AARP newsletter, February 2001: 18) wrote the new magazine's launch editor, a Boomer herself, who began a lead issue of *My Generation* in this way:

> It's our party! What is it about 50th birthdays that demands celebration?… There's no escaping the inevitable tangle of cosmic questions that seem to attach themselves to this birthday: What next? What kind of person will I be in this part of my life? How did this happen to me?… The good news is that you're not alone in this bewildering situation (there are 76 million of us). And now we have a new magazine, *My Generation*, that's just for us…. Before we began *My Generation* we did a lot of research and confirmed what we'd already suspected. This generation of ours refuses to believe it's getting older. How could we be old if we're still out there rollerblading and listening to Radiohead? 'I am not fifty like my parents were' was the refrain we heard from people across the country. We hope *My Generation* will become an indispensable resource guide for your life.[7]

It didn't. In less than a year, *My Generation* was closed down as a separate title, merging back into *Modern Maturity*, which was then re-launched as an all-cohort inclusive magazine with a new title, *AARP – The Magazine*. AARP declared that the change was based on the realization that 'what unites the generations is much more powerful than what separates us', especially in the wake of 9/11,[8] while media commentators attributed the closure to a lack of support among advertisers and Boomers alike.

Like the Lycra leggings that were not in the shops and the leotards and leggings that were not on the Lycra timeline, the missing midlife magazines are examples of stuff that isn't there, which takes us back to the heart of the ethnographic moment. Material culture – the study of society through stuff – presents a literal, explicit portrait of 'how things are', the 'natural' and taken-for-granted model of everyday life. But what is around us is only part of the story. There could have been other things, there may have been things once that are no longer there. Looking at stuff that isn't there – or stuff that should and could be there, or was there once but isn't now – gives a far more dynamic and nuanced view of society, process and changing ideologies and values than material culture alone. It allows us to look beneath the surface, to ask deeper questions about why things are the way they are. This does not diminish the study of stuff, but enhances it by giving it another dimension, leading to a deeper understanding of contemporary social processes and problems (Forman 1995). I thought of giving the study of stuff that isn't there a name of its own – possibly 'immaterial culture' – but 'immaterial' has too many competing meanings. Other possibilities were 'Invisible Culture' and 'Dark Material Culture', because the study of stuff that isn't there seemed to me very much like the study of dark matter, the invisible energy and matter that is thought to make up 80 percent of the universe, but whose presence can only be inferred from what can be seen. However, the approach introduced here remains simply 'the study of stuff that isn't there'. So – what does it show us?

In the 1960s, the Boomers created the new normativity of youth, which became deeply embedded in American society as an ideology and cultural value, given material form by the mass production and consumption of goods created for the new young consumers. Lycra leggings and leotards became associated with the values of a particular time and place, and with the cohort who wore them. As time went on, the positive cultural value placed on youth intensified, with a concomitant rise in negative attitudes to aging and to age. Material goods that had long been used to mark the social category of 'old', such as 'older women's dresses', disappeared. The cohort of Boomer women who didn't want to look like their mothers ended up wanting to look like their own daughters. Producers became accustomed to thinking of production primarily in terms of the youth market and, as they aged, the Boomers resisted consuming goods that would constitute them as 'no longer young'. Having been instrumental in creating this normativity of youth, producers and the aging Boomers became trapped in it. The absence of aerobic leotards and leggings on the Lycra timeline can be seen as a reflection of Dupont's predicament. The company had discovered that, due to symbolic processes and the power of culture, producers who are successful at building brand loyalty may find that very loyalty becomes problematic with time, identifying them with consumers and products that come to be seen as old-fashioned or simply 'old' in a society where youth and the new are celebrated, commercial death for a brand recently re-invented for the contemporary youth market. So the producers were struggling to escape leggings because of their association with age and the past, even as the Boomer woman of my ethnographic moment and countless others like her were struggling to acquire Lycra leggings, to recapture the past and reconstruct their youthful selves on many levels. Sahlins (1976: 384) had indeed been right when he wrote: 'Western capitalism in its totality is a truly exotic cultural scheme, as bizarre as any other ... we are too much misled by the apparent pragmatism of production and consumption. The whole cultural organization of our economy remains invisible.'

As I sat in the sunlight at Hagley, I tried to tie up the loose ends of the entwined life cycles of family, firm and fiber. Capitalism was indeed far more complex than the conventional political–economic model, and looking at Dupont through the stuff it produced and the way it transformed everyday life had resulted in a more nuanced and positive view of capitalism and corporations than is generally found in the academic literature. The Dupont family dynamic and myth that were central to the early history of the company and its transition to the corporate form were not as central to day-to-day operations as they had once been, but their continued presence as part of the company's public face show an enduring importance to the company, part of the way they see themselves. Following Lycra's paper trail demonstrated that archives are a valid ethnographic site and has also showed how collective representations of cohorts like the Boomers or Generation Y allow us to 'see' statistics, enabling anthropology to re-establish a more general level of understanding of the mainstream of the society in which we live. All in all, in the case of Lycra, anthropology and the study of stuff that wasn't there had provided a richer, more complex and more dynamic understanding than could be achieved through economic or business history, sociology, women's studies or cultural studies alone. And it had shown that commercial 'failures' have as much to tell us as the study of success. Multi-site studies find new paths and connections but don't follow them all up, while ethnographic moments start with answers and end with questions. Now there are new avenues to explore, new answers to be found, new questions to be asked, new studies to be carried out – cohort studies, studies that will give fuller historical, social and political context to Lycra than was possible here, studies that will fully explore Lycra from a feminist, gender and age perspective, studies of other kinds of stuff – and of stuff that isn't there.

I was sad when I walked away from the Brandywine that day, but I needn't have been. So much is happening, and there is so much yet to do. Today, under new ownership, Lycra is forging new youth markets in India, China and Brazil, sponsoring young fashion awards, building a lively digital presence and shaping new generations of bodies globally, a testament to Dupont and the Duponters who created and developed it, and to the vitality of the fiber itself. At home, the Sky reality TV show Pineapple Dance Studios with Debbie Moore is re-popularizing Lycra dance dressing, and Jane Fonda has launched new exercise DVDs aimed at Boomers. Maybe my Boomer shopper will get her leggings after all. This is not the end of the biography of Lycra. Despite producers and consumers, economy and demography, change and continuity, time and space – stuff has a life of its own.

NOTES

2 Dupont: Culture, Kinship and Myth

1 See Dell, John Edward (ed.) in association with Walt Reed 2000. *Visions of Adventure: N.C. Wyeth and the Brandywine Artists.* New York, Watson-Gupthill Publications.

2 In 2003, Johnson & Johnson heir Jamie Johnson created and directed an award-winning documentary, *Born Rich*, on the experience of growing up in wealthy American dynastic families such as the Newhouses (Conde Nast Publications), the Whitneys and the Vanderbilts. See http://hbo.com/docs/programs/born_rich/index.html.

3 Du Pont, Gabrielle Josephine de la Fite de Pelleport du Pont (de Nemours). (Madame Victor Marie du Pont de Nemours), 1826. *Our Transplantation to America.* Unpublished manuscript, Hagley Museum and Library.

4 See Irving, Washington 1987. *Astoria*, with an introduction by Kaori O'Connor. London and New York, KPI, Pacific Basin Books.

5 I am grateful to one of my anonymous reviewers for raising these further questions.

6 Sales Promotion Policy of Eleuthère Irénée Dupont 1804 and 1809. LMS/10/C, L54, Box 11, p. 4, Hagley Museum and Library.

7 *Rayon Yarns*, April 4, 1956, Hagley Museum and Library.

8 Brayman, Harold 1947. *The Organization of the Dupont Company*, Dupont Public Relations Dept., August 1947. Moosman. Acc 2106, p. 6, Hagley Museum and Library.

9 Brayman, Harold 1947. *The Organization of the Dupont Company*, Dupont Public Relations Dept., August 1947. Moosman. Acc 2106, p. 7, Hagley Museum and Library.

10 Brayman, Harold 1947. *The Organization of the Dupont Company*, Dupont Public Relations Dept., August 1947. Moosman. Acc 2106, p. 13, Hagley Museum and Library.

11 Brandywine River Museum, 2000. *The Du Pont Family: Two Hundred Years of Portraits.* Chadds Ford, Pennsylvania.

3 Dupont's Family of Fibers and the Birth of Lycra

1 Agulnick, Seth 2002. After a Bountiful History, Innovations Slow. *The News Journal*, Delaware, June 30, 2002.

2 Dupont Company 1965. *History of the Textile Fibers Department.* Acc 2215, Box 77, file Technological Information, Hagley Museum and Library.

3 Paint and anti-freeze, which Dupont sold to the public, were exceptions.

4 *Fiber Facts*, May 10, 1965, Hagley Museum and Library.

5 Excerpts from NBC News Broadcast from New York at 10:15 am, December 22, 1944 by Robert St John. Acc 2028, Nylon Notebook 1938–1963, Hagley Museum and Library.

6 *Dupont Magazine*, A Promise Made, A Promise Kept, November/December 1985, p. 14, Hagley Museum and Library.

7 *Rayon Yarns*, June 1948, Hagley Museum and Library.

8 I am grateful to one of my anonymous reviewers for drawing this parallel to my attention.

9 Dupont Company 1942. *The Historical and Art Significance of the Twelve Paintings in the du Pont Safety Calendar of 1942.* Pictorial Collections, Hagley Museum and Library.

10 Hobbs, G.D. 1952. *The Dress Industry.* Market Research Report, Textile Fibers Department, June 16, 1952, 1, Hagley Museum and Library.

11 Dupont Company. The 1970s. General Summary. Acc 2215, Box 77, File Technological Information, Hagley Museum and Library.

12 Colby, Anita. *Ideas from a Woman's Viewpoint.* Prepared for the Du Pont Advertising Clinic, May 26, 1955. Acc 1195, Series II, Pt 2, Box 76, Hagley Museum and Library.

13 Textile Fibers Product Information 1959, 84.259, Box 1, Hagley Museum and Library.

14 BBDO (Batten, Barton, Durstine & Osborn Inc) for E.I. Du Pont de Nemours & Co Inc. Cavalcade of America (TV), script #68. Acc 1803, Advertising, Soda House, Series I, Box 9, Hagley Museum and Library.

15 Cox, Mary Jane. *Women's Opinions of the First 'Du Pont Show' with June Allyson.* Marketing Research, Textile Fibers Department, October 20, 1959. MMR-59–51, p. 1, Hagley Museum and Library.

16 Linen, James A. Ideas in Publishing. Prepared for the 1955 Du Pont Advertising Clinic, May 26, 1955. Acc 1195, Sec II, Pt 2, Box 76, Hagley Museum and Library.

17 'Your Customer in a World of Change', Dupont Company, May 22, 1958. Acc 1195, Sec II, Pt 2, Box 78, Advertising 1946–69, 1958, Hagley Museum and Library.

18 Kluckhohn, Clyde. Changing Values, p. 6, prepared for the 1958 Dupont Advertising Forum. Acc 1195, Sec II, Pt 2, Box 78, Advertising 1946–69, Hagley Museum and Library.

19 Dupont/Marketing Research. Research Basis for the Self-Confidence Theme. Report MMR-59–33, 1959, Hagley Museum and Library.

20 Barnes, Edith 1959. *Orlon for Babies.* Textile Fibers Product Information 84.259, Box 1, Hagley Museum and Library.

21 *Dupont Magazine,* March 1936, Hagley Museum and Library.

22 Dupont, Pioneering Research Div. Acc 1771, Series I, Sub Sec A, Box 24, 1946, f27, 28, Hagley Museum and Library.

23 Dupont, Pioneering Research Div. Acc 1771, Series I, Sub Sec A, Box 24, 1946, f27, 28, Hagley Museum and Library.

24 Houtz, R.C. 1952. Pioneering Research Division, April 2. Acc 1771, Box 38, file PM1 Material General, Hagley Museum and Library.

25 Dupont Pioneering Research Div. Acc 1771, Box 41, Dec. 17, 1954, Hagley Museum and Library.

26 Elastomer and Chemical Spinning Patent Memorandum, Dec. 27, 1954. Acc 1771, Box 41, Hagley Museum and Library.

4 Launching Lycra

1 McCann-Erickson/Market Planning Corp. 1960. The Decade of Incentive: A Marketing Profile of 'The Big Sixties'. PAM, Hagley Museum and Library.

2 Brainstorming at Dupont. Acc 1803, Series I, Advertising, Box 27, Hagley Museum and Library.

3 McCormick, James H. 1956. Advertising Department Panel Chairman, Stretch Yarns. Brainstorming at Dupont. Acc 1803, Series I, Box 27, Hagley Museum and Library.

4 Report of Interview, Elastomers in Foundation Fabrics. Acc 1771, file PM4, Jan. 26, 1955, Hagley Museum and Library.

5 Ayer Marketing Research Report MMR-59–64, Final Report, Powernet Girdle Trial, December 30, 1959, Hagley Museum and Library.

6 Acc 500, Series II, Pt II, V613, p. 87, Box 43, Hagley Museum and Library.

7 *Fiber Facts* May 10, 1962, Hagley Museum and Library.

8 *Fiber Facts* February 16, 1961, Hagley Museum and Library.

9 *Fiber Facts* February 16, 1961, Hagley Museum and Library.

10 Pioneering Acc 1771, Box 38, file Material General, 1952, Hagley Museum and Library.

11 *Fiber Facts* May 10, 1962, original emphasis, Hagley Museum and Library.

12 *Fiber Facts* February 16, 1961, Hagley Museum and Library.

13 *Fiber Facts* February 16, 1961, Hagley Museum and Library.

14 *Dupont Magazine*, Vol. 54, No. 2, p. 4, Hagley Museum and Library.

15 *Fiber Facts* May 10, 1965, Hagley Museum and Library.

16 Textile Fibers Product Information. Acc 1771, Hagley Museum and Library.

17 Textile Fibers Product Information. Acc 1771, Hagley Museum and Library.

18 *Fiber Facts* May 10, 1962, Hagley Museum and Library.

19 Dupont, Rutledge Scrapbook. Acc 500, Sec II, Pt 2, V613, Hagley Museum and Library.

20 Dupont, *Selling Tips*. Rutledge Scrapbook. Acc 500, Sec II, Pt 2, V613, p. 127, Hagley Museum and Library.

21 Dupont, *The Adventures of Selma the Star Sales Girl*. Rutledge Scrapbook. Acc 500, Sec II, Pt 2, V613, Hagley Museum and Library.

22 Product Information Service. Acc 500, Series III, Pt 2, V63, Box 43, HML.

23 Product Information Service, Sept. 19, 1962. Acc 500, Series II, Pt 2, V63, p. 117, Box 43, Hagley Museum and Library.

24 *Dupont Magazine*, How You Help to Tailor Textiles. July/August 1960, p. 11, Hagley Museum and Library.

25 *Dupont Magazine*, The Golden Sixties: The Next Ten Years Promise Enormous Growth, Vol. 53, No. 5, pp. 2–6, Hagley Museum and Library.

26 National Analysts Inc. 1956. *Nylon Hosiery: A Study of the Consumer*. Textile Fibers Product Information 84.259, Box 29, my italics, Hagley Museum and Library.

27 *Dupont Magazine*, Teen Age Boom Rocks the Market, Vol. 59, No. 5, 1965, my italics, Hagley Museum and Library.

28 *Dupont Magazine*, Teen Age Boom Rocks the Market, Vol. 59, No. 5, 1965, Hagley Museum and Library.

29 *Dupont Magazine*, A Study in Gentle Persuasion: Promising Prospects for Semi-Control Garments of Lycra is One Forecast That Emerges from a Du Pont Scientist's Study. November/December, pp. 12–15, my italics, Hagley Museum and Library.

30 Weishar, Joseph. *The Hidden Market Potential in 'Control' Garments. A Research Study of Current Merchandising Trends Sponsored by Dupont*. TPFI 84.259, Box 21, Hagley Museum and Library.

31 Curtin, Jack. What's It All About?, *Better Living*, November/December 1969, Hagley Museum and Library.

32 Ernest Dichter Associates 1975. *A Motivational Research Study of the Sales Opportunities for Ladies' Girdles*, Hagley Museum and Library.

33 Brand Gruber and Co., June 1975 (Brand Gruber Pt 1), *A Limited Study of Retail Foundation Department Buyers and Managers, for E.I. du Point de Nemours Inc.* Textile Fibers Product Information 84.259, Box 25, p. 7, Hagley Museum and Library.

34 Brand Gruber Pt I, p. 12, Hagley Museum and Library.

35 Brand Gruber and Co., July 1975 (Brand Gruber Pt II), *Opportunities for the All-In-One Undergarments* for E.I. du Pont de Nemours Inc. Textile Fibers Product Information 84.259, Box 25, pp. 5, 14, Hagley Museum and Library.

36 Brand Gruber Pt II, p. 16, Hagley Museum and Library.

37 Lycra Idea Generation Meeting. Textile Fibers Product Information 84.259, Box 25, August 12, 1975, Hagley Museum and Library.

38 Haverfield, Kay 1976. Press release *Something New To Wear When Exercising: The Flexatard*. Textile Fibers Product Information 64.259, Box 56, December 1976, Hagley Museum and Library.

39 Dupont Fashion News – Women's Bodygarments Have Been Liberated Too. Textile Fibers Product Information, Box 26, Hagley Museum and Library.

40 Flynn Helen. Put On the Power. Textile Fibers Product Information 84.259, Box 57, February 1971, Hagley Museum and Library.

41 Weishar, Joseph. *The Hidden Market Potential in 'Control Garments'. A Research Study of Current Retail Merchandising Trends Sponsored by Du Pont.* Textile Fibers Product Information 84.249, Box 21, Hagley Museum and Library.

42 *Control Garments: Do They Have A Future?* Dupont. TPFI 84.259, Box 80, HML.

43 Textile Fibers Product Information 84.259, Box 27, Hagley Museum and Library.

44 Dupont. Acc 500, Series II, Pt 2, V613, p. 131, Box 43, Hagley Museum and Library.

45 Lycra Idea Generation Meeting. Textile Fibers Product Information 84.259, Box 25, August 12, 1975, Hagley Museum and Library.

5 Lycra, Aerobics and the Rise of the Legging

1 Lycra Idea Generation Meeting. Textile Fiber Product Information 84.259, Box 25, August 12, 1975, Hagley Museum and Library.

2 Haverfield, Kay. Press release, December 27, 1976, Textile Fiber Product Information 84.259, Hagley Museum and Library.

3 Haverfield, Kay. Dupont Fashion News. First Role for Disco Dressing: Look Right. August 28, 1978. Textile Fiber Product Information 84.259, Box 62, file 338, 1978 master, Hagley Museum and Library.

4 Herbert E. Mecke Associates Inc., Quantitative Assessment of the Market for Leotards and Related Garments, Marketing Research Division, PG82–228, March 1983, Hagley Museum and Library.

5 Brigham, R.T. 1985. Retail Sales – Women's Leotards. 1984 Profile. April, Textile Marketing Division, Textile Fibers Department, Hagley Museum and Library.

6 In Brigham 1985.

7 E.I. du Pont de Nemours & Co (Inc.) 1985. *Leotards: Poised for Growth or Fashion Fad?* Hagley Museum and Library.

8 BASF Fibers Market Research Services. Women's Sheer Hosiery: Industry, Products, Markets. TPFI Hosiery File, February 26, 1986, F.G. Oswald, Hagley Museum and Library.

9 Bishop, Audrey. Stretch Corps. Textile Fibers Product Information. Acc 500, Series II, Pt 2, V63, p. 117, Box 43, Hagley Museum and Library.

10 Dupont press release. *The Working Woman is Fashion's Greatest Challenge.* Textile Fibers Product Information 84.259, Box 62, July 1978, Hagley Museum and Library.

11 Acc 500, Sec II, Pt 2, V613, p. 122, Rutledge scrapbook, Hagley Museum and Library.

12 Dupont Fashion News: Blend Denim of Cotton and Dacron Polyester. Textile Fibers Product Information, Eleanor Walsh, 1979, Hagley Museum and Library.

13 Brigham, R.T. 1982. A Report of Research: Further Consumer Reaction to Jeans with Lycra, August. Marketing Research Division PG82–174, Hagley Museum and Library.

14 Brand, Gruber and Company for E.I. Du Pont de Nemours & Co Inc., *Optimizing Market for Lycra Panties and Lycra Pantyhose.* PG 82–214, September 1982, p. 14, Hagley Museum and Library.

15 Ibrahim, Salim. Quoted in *The Free-Lance Star,* June 29, 1995.

16 Ibid.

17 *Dupont Magazine,* No. 3, 12–14, 1999, Selling the Invisible Difference, Hagley Museum and Library.

18 *Dupont Magazine,* July/August 1996, Spinning Thread into Gold, Hagley Museum and Library.

19 Results derived from an online 1999 survey conducted by Dryel and the Council of Fashion Designers of America, to which 14,000 people responded, author's collection.

20 BBDO, H.L. Blackburn, letter to F.L. Dewey, Advertising, Dupont, April 28, 1947. Acc 641, Box 33/75, file 1947, Hagley Museum and Library.

21 www.greatdayamerica.com/style/hot/lycra-40th, accessed November 15, 2002.

22 Kearns, Linda, in www.greatdayamerica.com/style/hot/lycra-40th, accessed November 15, 2002

23 *Cosmo Girl*, a spin-off of *Cosmopolitan* magazine, was launched in 1999 and ceased publication in December 2008.

24 www.lycra.com/lycra/news/dupont in the news/brandweek, accessed November 15, 2002.

25 www.dupont.com/corp/news/product/2002, Lycra Plays Key Role in Revitalization of Denim, accessed November 15, 2002.

26 www.lycrateens.com, accessed February 3, 1999.

27 www.dupont.com, accessed February 1998.

28 www.lycra.com, accessed February 18, 2003.

29 Braus, Patricia. Boomers Against Gravity. *American Demographics* February 1995, p. 55.

30 Ibid., p. 50.

31 Ibid., p. 54.

32 www.augustachronicle.com, 2003.

33 In Hinds, Julie 1997. The Shape of Things to Come. *The Detroit News*, February 7.

34 In Braus, 1995.

35 D'Innocenzio, Anne 2003. *Associated Press*, January 16.

36 Dupont press release, autumn/winter 1999/2000, author's collection.

37 Lycra/Corporate Concepts 1975, Hagley Museum and Library.

38 *Dupont Magazine*, The Shape of Things to Come. March/April 1996, Hagley Museum and Library.

39 *Lycra: the Past, Present and Future of Fashion.* Dupont press release, 2000, author's collection.

6 Another Ethnographic Moment

1 Chembytes e-zine 2002. *Dupont Steps into a New Era.* www.chemsoc.org/chembytes/ezine.2002/stevenson_aug02, accessed December 2, 2002.

2 In 2004, Dupont sold Invista, its re-named spun-off Textile Division, to Koch Industries, Inc.

3 www.dupont.com, accessed March 6, 2002.

4 Agulnick, Seth 2002. After a Bountiful History, Innovations Slow. *The News Journal*, Delaware, June 30.

5 Milford, Maureen 2002. Nurturing Climate Fell Prey to Changing Times. *The News Journal*, Delaware, June 30.

6 Agulnick, Seth 2002. After a Bountiful History, Innovations Slow. *The News Journal*, Delaware, June 30.

7 Carter, Betsy 2002. *My Generation*, March–April, p. 1.

8 Delhanty, Hugh 2003. *AARP – The Magazine*, March/April, p. 6.

REFERENCES

Anderson, Ronald C. and David M. Reeb 2003. Founding Family Ownership and Firm Performance: Evidence from the S&P Index. *The Journal of Finance*, Vol. LVIII, No. 3, June.

Appadurai, Arjun 1986. Introduction: Commodities and the Politics of Value. In Appadurai, Arjun (ed.) *The Social Life of Things*. Cambridge, Cambridge University Press, pp. 3–63.

Barthes, Roland 1985. *The Fashion System*. London, Jonathan Cape.

Bercovici, Jeff 2003. From My Generation to AARP The Magazine. *Media Life* January.

Blanchard, Kendall 1995. *The Anthropology of Sport*. Westport and London, Bergin and Garvey.

Blaszczyk, Regina Lee 2006. Styling Synthetics: Dupont's Marketing of Fabrics and Fashions in Postwar America. *Business History Review* 80, autumn 2006, pp. 485–528.

Blaszczyk, Regina Lee 2009. *American Consumer Society 1865–2005: From Hearth to HDTV*. Wheeling, Harlan Davidson Inc.

Bloch, Maurice 1977. The Past and the Present in the Present. *Man* Vol. 12, No. 2, pp. 278–292.

Boston Women's Health Collective 1973. *Our Bodies, Our Selves*. Boston, Boston Women's Health Collective.

Bourdieu, Pierre 1977. *Outline of a Theory of Practice*. Cambridge, Cambridge University Press.

Brandes, Stanley 1985. *Forty: The Age and the Symbol*. Knoxville, University of Tennessee Press.

Brandes, Stuart 1976. *American Welfare Capitalism 1880–1940*. Chicago, University of Chicago Press.

Carr, William H.A. 1965. *The Duponts of Delaware*. London, Frederick Muller.

Catanese, Lynn Ann 1997. *Women's History: A Guide to Sources at Hagley Museum and Library*. Westport, Greenwood Press.

Chandler, Alfred D. Jr. 1972. *Strategy and Structure: Chapters in the History of the American Industrial Enterprise*. Boston, MIT Press.

Chandler, Alfred D. Jr. 1978. *The Visible Hand: The Managerial Revolution in American Business*. Harvard, The Belknap Press.

Chandler, Alfred D. Jr. and Stephen Salisbury 1971. *Pierre du Pont and the Making of the Modern Corporation*. New York, Harper and Row.

Comaroff, John and Jean Comaroff 1992. *Ethnography and the Historical Imagination*. Boulder, Westview Press.

Crippen, Kaye with Pauline Tng and Patricia Mulready 1995. Dupont Shifts Emphasis to Global Brand Management. *Journal of Product and Brand Management* Vol. 4, No. 3, 1995, pp. 27–37.

Cross, Gary 2000. *An All-Consuming Century: Why Commercialism Won in Modern America*. New York, Columbia University Press.

Deal, Terrence and Allen Kennedy 1982. *Corporate Cultures: The Rites and Rituals of Corporate Life*. London, Penguin Books.

Donohue, John J. 1993. The Ritual Dimension of Karate-Do. *Journal of Ritual Studies* Vol. 7: No. 1.

Douglas, Mary 1978. *Cultural Bias.* Royal Anthropological Institute Occasional Paper No. 35. London.

Douglas, Mary 1992. *Risk and Blame: Essays in Cultural Theory.* London and New York, Routledge.

Douglas, Mary 1996. *Natural Symbols: Explorations in Cosmology.* London and New York, Routledge.

Douglas, Mary and Baron Isherwood 1996. *The World of Goods: Towards an Anthropology of Consumption.* London and New York, Routledge.

Drucker-Brown, Susan 1997. Comments on Nader, Laura 1997. Controlling Processes: Tracing the Dynamic Components of Power. *Current Anthropology* Vol. 18, No. 1, December, p. 727.

Dupont, Pierre Samuel 1984. *The Autobiography of Du Pont de Nemours.* Translated and with an Introduction by Elizabeth Fix-Genovese. Wilmington, Delaware, Scholarly Resources Inc.

DuPont Company (E.I. du Pont de Nemours and Company) 1952. *DuPont: The Autobiography of an American Enterprise.* Wilmington, Delaware, E.I. du Pont de Nemours and Company.

Dutton, William S. 1942. *Du Pont: One Hundred and Forty Years.* New York, Scribners.

Firth, Raymond with Jane Hubert and Anthony Forge 1969. *Families and their Relatives: Kinship in a Middle-Class Sector of London.* London, Routledge and Kegan Paul.

Fonda, Jane 1981. *Jane Fonda's Workout Book.* New York, Simon and Schuster.

Forman, Shepard 1995. Introduction. In Forman, Shepard (ed.) *Diagnosing America: Linking Levels of Analysis.* Ann Arbor, University of Michigan Press.

Geertz, Clifford 1973. *The Interpretation of Cultures.* New York, Basic Books.

Granskog, Jane E. 1993. In Search of the Ultimate: Aspects of the Hawaiian Ironman Triathlon. *Journal of Ritual Studies* Vol. 7, No. 1, pp. 3–25.

Green, Harvey 1986. *Fit for America.* Baltimore and London, Johns Hopkins University Press.

Gunther, John 1947. *Inside America.* New York, Harper Brothers.

Handley, Susannah 1999. *Nylon and the Man-Made Fashion Revolution: A Celebration from Art Silk to Nylon and Thinking Fibres.* London, Bloomsbury.

Hansen, Karen Tranberg 2004. The World in Dress: Anthropological Perspectives on Clothing, Fashion and Culture. *Annual Review of Anthropology 2004*, pp. 369–392.

Hardy, Stephen 1990. Entrepreneurs, Structures and the Sportgeist: Old Tensions in a Modern Industry. In Kyle, Donald G. and Stark, Gary D. (eds.) *Essays on Sport History and Sport Mythology.* College Station, Texas, A&M University Press.

Hollander, Stanley and Richard Germain 1992. *Was There a Pepsi Generation Before Pepsi Discovered It? Youth-Based Segmentation Marketing.* Lincolnwood, NTC Business Books.

Holmes, Frederic L. 1990. Laboratory Notebooks: Can the Daily Record Illuminate the Broader Picture? *Proceedings of the American Philosophical Society* Vol. 134, No. 4, December 1990, pp. 349–366.

Holt, Douglas B. 2004. *How Brands Become Icons: The Principles of Cultural Branding.* Boston, Harvard Business School Press.

Hounshell, David A. 1990. Interpreting the History of Industrial Research and Development. The Case of E.I. du Pont de Nemours & Company. *Proceedings of the American Philosophical Society* Vol. 134, No. 4, pp. 387–407.

Hounshell, David A. and John Kenly Smith Jr. 1988a. The Nylon Drama. *American Heritage Invention and Technology Magazine* Fall 1988, pp. 40–55. Online: http://invention.smithsonian.org/centerpieces/whole_cloth/u7sf/u7materials/nylondrama.html.

Hounshell, David A. and John Kenly Smith Jr. 1988b. *Science and Corporate Strategy: Du Pont R&D 1902–1980.* Cambridge and New York, Cambridge University Press.

Hymes, Dell 1972. The Use of Anthropology: Critical, Political and Personal. In Hymes, Dell (ed.) *Reinventing Anthropology.* New York, Pantheon Books.

Kammen, Michael 1987. *Selvages & Biases: The Fabric of History in American Culture.* Ithaca and London, Cornell University Press.

Kammen, Michael 1999. *American Culture, American Tastes: Social Change and the 20th Century.* New York, Basic Books.

Keith, Jennie and David I. Kertzer 1984. Introduction. In Kertzer, David I and Keith, Jennie (eds.) *Age and Anthropological Theory.* Ithaca, Cornell University Press.

Kenis, Patrick 1992. *The Social Construction of an Industry: A World of Chemical Fibers.* Campus Verlag/Frankfurt-am-Main with Westview Press, Boulder.

Kertzer, David I. and Howard Fricke (eds.) 1997. *Anthropological Demography: Toward a New Synthesis.* Chicago, University of Chicago Press.

Kinnane, Adrian 2002. *DuPont: From the Banks of the Brandywine to Miracles of Science.* Wilmington, E.I. du Pont de Nemours and Company.

Koehn, Nancy 2001. *Brand New: How Entrepreneurs Earned Consumers' Trust from Wedgwood to Dell.* Boston, Harvard Business School Press.

Kopytoff, Igor 1986. The Cultural Biography of Things: Commoditization As Process. In Appadurai, Arjun (ed.) *The Social Life of Things.* Cambridge, Cambridge University Press.

Kuper, Adam 2001. Fraternity and Endogamy: The House of Rothschild. *Social Anthropology* Vol. 8, No. 3, pp. 273–287.

Lakoff, Robin Tolmach and R.L. Scherr 1984. *Face Value: The Politics of Beauty.* London and Boston, Routledge and Kegan Paul.

Lanagan, David 2002. Surfing in the Third Millennium: Commodifying the Visual Argot. *The Australian Journal of Anthropology* Vol. 13, No. 3, pp. 283–291.

Lears, Jackson 1994. *Fables of Abundance: A Cultural History of Advertising in America.* New York, Basic Books.

Leonard, Annie 2007. *The Story of Stuff.* www.thestoryofstuff.com, accessed December 2009.

Levi-Strauss, Claude 1963. *Structural Anthropology.* New York, Basic Books.

Lewis, I.M. 1989. *Ecstatic Religion: A Study of Shamanism and Spirit Possession* (second edition). London and New York, Routledge.

Lock Margaret 1993a. The Politics of Mid-Life and Menopause: Ideologies for the Second Sex in North America and Japan. In Lindenbaum, Shirley and Lock, Margaret (eds.) *Knowledge, Power and Practice: The Anthropology of Medicine and Everyday Life.* Berkeley, University of California Press.

Lock, Margaret 1993b. *Encounters with Aging: Mythologies of Menopause in Japan and North America.* Berkeley, University of California Press.

Lock, Margaret 1999. Cultivating the Body: Anthropology and the Epistemologies of Bodily Practice. *Annual Review of Anthropology* Vol. 22, pp. 133–155.

McCracken, Grant 1988. *Culture and Consumption: New Approaches to the Symbolic Character of Consumer Goods and Activities.* Bloomington, Indiana University Press.

McCracken, Grant D. and Richard W. Pollay 1981. *Anthropology and the Study of Advertising.* Working Paper 815. History of Advertising Archives, Faculty of Commerce and Business Administration, University of British Columbia.

MacLennan, Carol 1995. Democratic Participation: A View From Anthropology. In Forman, Shepard (ed.) *Diagnosing America: Linking Levels of Analysis.* Ann Arbor, University of Michigan Press.

McMillan, G. Steven and Diana Hicks 2001. Science and Corporate Strategy: A Bibliometric Update of Hounshell and Smith. *Technology Analysis and Strategic Management* Vol. 13, No. 4, pp. 497–505.

Maguire, Jennifer Smith 2007. *Fit for Consumption: Sociology and the Business of Fitness.* London and New York, Routledge.

Marchand, Roland 1985. *Advertising the American Dream: Making Way for Modernity 1920–1940.* Berkeley and London, University of California Press.

Marchand, Roland 1998. *Creating the Corporate Soul: The Rise of Public Relations and Corporate Imagery in American Big Business.* Berkeley and London, University of California Press.

Marcus, George E. 1994. After the Critique of Anthropology. In Borofsky, Robert (ed.) *Assessing Cultural Anthropology.* New York and London, McGraw Hill.

Marcus, George E. 1995. Ethnography In/Of the World System: the Emergence of Multi-Sited Ethnography. *Annual Review of Anthropology 1995* 24, pp. 95–117.

Marcus, George E. 1998. *Ethnography Through Thick and Thin.* Princeton, Princeton University Press.

Marcus, George E. with Peter Dobkin Hall 1992. *Lives in Trust: The Fortunes of Dynastic Families in Late Twentieth Century America.* Boulder, Westview Press.

Martin, Emily 1994. *Flexible Bodies: Tracking Immunity in American Culture, From the Days of Polio to the Age of Aids.* Boston, Beacon Press.

Mead, Margaret and Rhoda Métraux (eds.) 1953. *The Study of Culture at a Distance.* Chicago, University of Chicago Press.

Merser, Cheryl 1987. *'Grown-Ups': A Generation in Search of Adulthood.* New York, G.P. Putnam's Sons.

Mewett, Peter 2002. Discourses of Deception: Cheating in Professional Running. *Australian Journal of Anthropology* Vol. 13, No. 3, pp. 292–308.

Miner, Horace 1956. Body Ritual Among the Nacirema. *American Anthropologist* 58, pp. 503–507.

Mintz, Sidney W. 1985. *Sweetness and Power: The Place of Sugar in Modern History.* New York, Viking Press.

Moore, Debbie 1983. *The Pineapple Dance Book.* London, Pavilion/Michael Joseph.

Moore, Sally Falke and Barbara G. Myerhoff (eds.) 1977. *Secular Ritual.* Assen, Van Gorcum.

Nader, Laura 1972. Up the Anthropologist. In Hymes, Dell (ed.) *Reinventing Anthropology.* New York, Pantheon Books.

Nader, Laura 1997. Controlling Processes: Tracing the Dynamic Components of Power. *Current Anthropology* Vol. 18, No. 5.

Noble, David F. 1977. *America by Design: Science, Technology and the Rise of Corporate Capitalism.* New York, Alfred A. Knopf.

Oakley, J. Ronald 1990. *God's Country: America in the 1950's.* New York, W.W. Norton.

O'Barr, William M. 1994. *Culture and the Ad: Exploring Otherness in the World of Advertising.* Boulder and London, Westview Press.

O'Connor, Kaori 2005. The Other Half: The Material Culture of New Fibers. In Kuchler, Susanne and Daniel Miller 2005. *Clothing as Material Culture.* Oxford and New York, Berg.

O'Connor, Kaori 2008. The Body and the Brand: How Lycra Shaped America. In Blaszczyk, Regina Lee (ed.) *Producing Fashion: Commerce, Culture and Consumers.* Philadelphia, University of Pennsylvania Press.

Ortner, Sherry B. 1984. Theory in Anthropology Since the Sixties. *Society for the Comparative Study of Society and History* Vol. 26, No. 1, pp. 126–166.

Ortner, Sherry B. 1999. Generation X: Anthropology in a Media-Saturated World. In Marcus, George (ed.) *Critical Anthropology Now.* Santa Fe, School of American Research Press.

Ortner, Sherry B. 2003, *New Jersey Dreaming: Capital, Culture, and the Class of '58.* Durham and London: Duke University Press.

Packard, Vance 1957. *The Hidden Persuaders.* New York, Pocket Books.

Palmer, Catherine 2002. Introduction: Anthropology and Sport. *The Australian Journal of Anthropology* Vol. 13, No. 3, p. 256.

Pollitt, Christopher 2000. Institutional Amnesia – A Paradox of the Information Age? *Prometheus* Vol. 18, No. 1, pp. 5–16.

Potter, David 1954. *People of Plenty: Economic Abundance and the American Character*. Chicago, Phoenix Books/University of Chicago Press.

Rayner, S. 1992. Cultural Theory and Risk Analysis. In Krimsky, S. and D. Golding (eds.) *Social Theories of Risk*. Santa Barbara, Greenwood Press, pp. 83–115.

Reingold, Nathan 1990. Tales from the Archives. *Proceedings of the American Philosophical Society* Vol. 134, No. 4, December, pp. 340–348.

Robbins, Richard H. 2006. *Cultural Anthropology: A Problem-Based Approach*. Belmont and London, Wadsworth Thomson.

Robbins, Richard H. 2011. *Global Problems and the Culture of Capitalism*. Upper Saddle River, New Jersey, Pearson Education.

Roberts, John G. 1983. *Mitsui: Three Centuries of Japanese Business*. New York and London, Weatherhill.

Robertson, Laurel with Carol Flinders and Bronwen Godfrey 1976. *Laurel's Kitchen*. Berkeley, Nilgiri Press.

Rumm, John C. 1989. *Mutual Interests: Managers and Workers at the Du Pont Company, 1802–1915*. Unpublished PhD dissertation, Hagley Museum and Library.

Sahlins, Marshall 1961. The Segmentary Lineage: An Organization of Predatory Expansion. *American Anthropologist* Vol. 63, pp. 322–345.

Sahlins, Marshall 1976. *Culture and Practical Reason*. Chicago, University of Chicago Press.

Sahlins, Marshall 1999. Two or Three Things I Know About Culture. *Journal of the Royal Anthropological Institute* Vol. 5, No. 3, September, pp. 399–421.

Schneider, Jane 1994. In and Out of Polyester: Desire, Disdain and Global Fibre Competitions. *Anthropology Today* Vol. 10, No. 4, August, pp. 2–10.

Smith, J. Walker and Ann Clurman 1997. *Rocking the Ages: The Yankelovich Report on Generational Marketing*. New York, HarperCollins.

Thompson, Michael with Richard J. Ellis and Aaron Wildavsky 1990. *Cultural Theory*. Boulder, Westview Press.

Tylor, Edward B. 1873. *Primitive Culture*. London, John Murray.

Veblen, Thorsten 1953. *Theory of the Leisure Class*. London, Macmillan.

Walker, Nancy 2000. *Shaping Our Mothers' World: American Women's Magazines*. Jackson, University of Mississippi Press.

Weiner, Annette and Jane Schneider (eds.) 1989. *Cloth and Human Experience*. Washington, DC, Smithsonian Institution Press.

Wolf, Roberta and Trudy Schlachter 2000. *Millennium Mode: Fashion Forecasts from 40 Top Designers*. New York, Rizzoli.

Yanagisako, Sylvia Junko 2002. *Producing Culture and Capital: Family Firms in Italy*. Princeton and Oxford, Princeton University Press.

Yanagisako, Sylvia Junko and Carol Delaney (eds.) 1994. *Naturalizing Power: Essays in Feminist Cultural Analysis*. London and New York, Routledge.

Zukin, Sharon 2004. *Point of Purchase: How Shopping Changed American Culture*. New York and London, Routledge.

INDEX

Note: locators in **bold** type indicate figures or illustrations, those in *italics* indicate tables.